# Cybersecurity Careers

*The Path to Becoming an Ethical Hacker or Analyst Break into one of the fastest-growing fields in tech*

THOMPSON CARTER

Table of Content

# *TABLE OF CONTENTS*

# Introduction

## Cybersecurity Careers: The Path to Becoming an Ethical Hacker or Analyst

In today's digitally driven world, the importance of cybersecurity cannot be overstated. With the ever-increasing volume and sophistication of cyberattacks, the demand for skilled cybersecurity professionals is higher than ever before. From protecting sensitive data to securing complex networks and critical infrastructures, cybersecurity professionals play a crucial role in safeguarding the digital world. The path to becoming an ethical hacker or security analyst offers an exciting and rewarding career for those passionate about technology, problem-solving, and making a real impact in the fight against cybercrime.

This book, **"Cybersecurity Careers: The Path to Becoming an Ethical Hacker or Analyst"**, is designed to provide a comprehensive guide to anyone seeking to break into or advance in the field of cybersecurity. Whether you're a beginner considering a career change or an experienced professional looking to refine your skills and progress to higher positions, this book offers valuable insights, practical advice, and real-world examples of how to build a successful career in cybersecurity.

**What You'll Learn**

This book will guide you through the entire journey of pursuing a career in cybersecurity, with a special focus on ethical hacking and security analysis. It will equip you with the knowledge to navigate the cybersecurity landscape, understand the various career paths, and take the necessary steps to develop the skills needed to succeed.

- **Emerging Trends in Cybersecurity**: You will gain an understanding of the latest trends and challenges shaping the cybersecurity field, including cloud security, IoT security, and the rise of quantum computing. This knowledge is essential for staying ahead in a constantly evolving industry.
- **Skills and Certifications**: We will explore the key skills required for cybersecurity professionals and dive into the certifications that can help you advance your career. From foundational certifications like **CompTIA Security+** to more advanced credentials like **CISSP** and **Certified Ethical Hacker (CEH)**,

we'll help you understand the value of these certifications and how to pursue them effectively.

- **Real-World Scenarios**: To help you apply your knowledge, we'll explore real-world examples of cybersecurity breaches, ethical dilemmas, and the roles that professionals play in both preventing and responding to cyber incidents. These scenarios will give you a deeper understanding of the challenges faced by cybersecurity experts and how they solve complex security issues.

- **Career Path Progression**: Whether you're starting as a junior analyst or aiming for the top role as a **CISO**, this book will help you map out a clear career progression. You will learn how to gain hands-on experience, improve your technical and soft skills, and work your way up to leadership positions in cybersecurity.

- **How to Transition into Cybersecurity**: If you're coming from a different field, this book will provide guidance on how to make a successful transition into cybersecurity, whether through self-study, formal education, or leveraging your previous professional experiences.

**Why Cybersecurity?**

The rapid digital transformation has led to an increasing number of businesses and individuals relying on technology, creating a growing attack surface for cybercriminals. As more critical data, financial transactions, and services move online, the threat of cyberattacks becomes more imminent, posing significant risks to businesses, governments, and individuals alike.

The COVID-19 pandemic accelerated this trend, with remote work and digital interactions becoming the norm for millions of people worldwide. Consequently, the cybersecurity field has seen a **significant surge in demand** for skilled professionals who can defend against a wide array of evolving threats.

Cybersecurity is not just a technical job; it's a **mission-critical field** where your work directly impacts the safety, privacy, and security of others. Whether it's protecting financial data, securing healthcare information, or ensuring national security, cybersecurity professionals are at the front lines, helping to safeguard the digital world.

**Who Should Read This Book?**

This book is for anyone interested in pursuing a career in cybersecurity, whether you are:

- A **beginner** looking to explore the field of cybersecurity and learn how to get started as an ethical hacker or security analyst.
- An **entry-level professional** seeking to build your career in cybersecurity and advance to higher positions.
- A **mid-career professional** aiming to shift to cybersecurity or refine your skills and expertise in a specific area (e.g., penetration testing, cloud security, incident response).
- Someone interested in the **ethical** aspects of hacking and how to contribute positively to the security landscape by becoming a certified ethical hacker or analyst.

**Why Ethical Hacking and Security Analysis?**

While cybersecurity as a whole is an essential industry, **ethical hacking** and **security analysis** are perhaps the most exciting and impactful areas within the field. As an ethical hacker, your job is to think like a cybercriminal—but for the greater good. You'll use your skills to identify weaknesses before malicious hackers can exploit them, often preventing devastating breaches and data losses.

Security analysts, on the other hand, work on the front lines, monitoring systems, analyzing data, and responding to potential threats in real-time. Both roles offer **intellectual stimulation**, the opportunity to solve complex problems, and the ability to make a tangible difference in the security and privacy of organizations worldwide.

By pursuing a career as an ethical hacker or security analyst, you're stepping into a profession that is not only highly rewarding but also offers **unparalleled job security**, with **skyrocketing demand** for skilled professionals in the cybersecurity space.

**A Comprehensive Guide to Cybersecurity Careers**

In this book, we've designed each chapter to be a step-by-step guide for building a career in cybersecurity. Starting with an overview of what ethical hacking and security analysis are, we will explore:

- The skills, certifications, and hands-on experience you need to succeed.

- The ethical and legal frameworks governing cybersecurity.
- Career paths and strategies for advancing to senior roles such as **CISO** or even running your own cybersecurity consultancy.
- Real-world case studies and success stories that will motivate and guide you as you progress in your cybersecurity career.

## Conclusion: The Journey Ahead

Cybersecurity is an exciting and fulfilling career path, offering endless opportunities for growth, development, and impact. Whether you're a beginner or an experienced professional, this book will provide the knowledge and tools you need to succeed. The world of cybersecurity is vast, and with the right skills and mindset, you can carve out a successful career while contributing to the protection and security of the digital world.

This is your roadmap to navigating the dynamic and ever-evolving field of cybersecurity. Let's dive into the world of ethical hacking and security analysis and start building your path to success.

---

This introduction provides a glimpse into the content of the book, offering insights into the journey of becoming a cybersecurity professional and highlighting the importance of cybersecurity in today's digital landscape. Let me know if you'd like further adjustments or additions!

# CHAPTER 1

# INTRODUCTION TO CYBERSECURITY

## Overview of the Cybersecurity Landscape

Cybersecurity is the practice of protecting systems, networks, and programs from **digital attacks**, damage, or unauthorized access. In today's interconnected world, where nearly every aspect of our lives is reliant on digital technologies, cybersecurity has become a critical component of daily operations for businesses, governments, and individuals alike. The digital landscape is constantly evolving, and as technology advances, so too do the methods used by malicious actors to exploit vulnerabilities.

Cyber threats can take many forms, including **malware**, **ransomware**, **phishing attacks**, **data breaches**, and **denial-of-service (DoS) attacks**, to name a few. These threats are not only growing in number but also in sophistication. Cybercriminals are increasingly using **AI**, **machine learning**, and **social engineering** tactics to bypass security measures and gain unauthorized access to sensitive data.

19

As businesses and individuals rely more heavily on digital infrastructure, the need for cybersecurity professionals who can anticipate, identify, and defend against these threats has never been greater.

**The Role of Cybersecurity in Protecting Businesses, Individuals, and Critical Infrastructure**

Cybersecurity plays a vital role in safeguarding the digital assets that businesses, governments, and individuals depend on. With the constant influx of data being exchanged across the internet and other digital channels, it is crucial to implement robust cybersecurity measures to ensure privacy, integrity, and security.

1. **Protecting                    Businesses**

   For businesses, cybersecurity protects everything from customer data to proprietary intellectual property. With online transactions, cloud services, and email communications, businesses are especially vulnerable to cyberattacks. Cybercriminals often target financial information, employee data, and

20

business operations to steal money, trade secrets, or disrupt day-to-day activities.

*Example*: In **2017**, the global shipping giant **Maersk** was hit by the **NotPetya ransomware attack**, resulting in widespread disruptions across their ports, terminals, and offices. The attack was estimated to cost the company upwards of **$300 million** in lost revenue and recovery costs. This attack illustrates how businesses that fail to adequately safeguard their digital infrastructure are at risk of catastrophic financial losses.

2. **Protecting                    Individuals**

Individuals are increasingly becoming targets of cybercriminals through tactics like **phishing** emails, **identity theft**, and **financial fraud**. From banking credentials to social security numbers, cybercriminals are eager to steal personal information for profit. Ensuring that individuals have proper defenses, such as strong passwords and encryption, is key to protecting their private data.

*Example*: In **2017**, the personal data of over **143 million Americans** was compromised in the

**Equifax data breach**. Hackers exploited a vulnerability in the company's systems and gained access to sensitive personal data, including social security numbers, addresses, and birth dates. The breach not only affected individuals' privacy but also led to significant reputational damage and financial penalties for Equifax.

3. **Protecting Critical Infrastructure**

Critical infrastructure refers to the essential systems that support the functioning of a society, such as electricity grids, water supply systems, healthcare networks, and transportation systems. These infrastructures are increasingly becoming digitized, making them susceptible to cyberattacks that can cause significant damage to public safety and national security.

*Example*: In **2015**, a cyberattack on Ukraine's **electric grid** left **230,000 people** without power for several hours. The attack was attributed to Russian-backed hackers and was one of the first publicly known instances of a **nation-state** using cyberattacks to disrupt critical infrastructure. Such attacks highlight the potential danger to governments and public services when cybersecurity is not prioritized.

---

**Real-World Examples of Significant Cybersecurity Breaches**

1. **The Equifax Breach (2017)** The **Equifax breach** remains one of the largest and most damaging data breaches in history. Hackers exploited a vulnerability in a web application used by Equifax to gain access to the personal information of 143 million Americans. The breach included names, social security numbers, birth dates, addresses, and even driver's license numbers. The fallout from this breach was catastrophic, with Equifax facing **$700 million** in settlement costs and a loss of consumer trust.

2. **The WannaCry Ransomware Attack (2017)** The **WannaCry** ransomware attack affected hundreds of thousands of computers across 150 countries. It exploited a vulnerability in **Windows operating systems**, locking users out of their files and demanding a ransom payment. The attack caused

widespread disruption, including halting critical services like the **National Health Service (NHS)** in the UK. WannaCry demonstrated the devastating effects of ransomware on both businesses and public services, highlighting the importance of keeping systems up-to-date with security patches.

3. **Target Data Breach (2013)** In **2013**, hackers gained access to **Target's** network through a third-party vendor and stole **40 million credit and debit card numbers** from customers. The breach also included **70 million records** of personal information, such as phone numbers and email addresses. The attack cost Target over **$200 million** in settlements and remediation efforts. This breach underscored the vulnerability of companies to third-party risks and the need for a layered cybersecurity approach.

## Why Cybersecurity is One of the Fastest-Growing Fields in Tech

The demand for cybersecurity professionals has skyrocketed in recent years, making it one of the fastest-growing fields in technology. This growth is driven by several factors:

1. **Increasing Cyber Threats**

   As the number and sophistication of cyber threats rise, businesses and governments are investing heavily in cybersecurity to safeguard their assets and protect sensitive information. According to the **Cybersecurity Ventures 2020 Report**, the global cost of cybercrime is expected to reach **$10.5 trillion annually** by **2025**. As a result, companies are scrambling to hire skilled professionals to combat this growing threat.

2. **Skills Gap and Demand for Talent**

   The cybersecurity field is experiencing a significant **skills gap**. According to the **International Information System Security Certification Consortium (ISC)²**, there were over **3 million unfilled cybersecurity positions** globally in 2020. This shortage of skilled workers has created abundant job opportunities for those looking to enter the field.

3. **Regulatory Pressures**

   Governments are implementing stricter regulations around data protection and privacy, such as the **General Data Protection Regulation (GDPR)** in the European Union. Companies are now required to comply with these regulations, creating a need for experts who can ensure that organizations meet the necessary standards. As cybersecurity threats and regulations continue to evolve, the demand for cybersecurity talent will only grow.

## The Importance of Ethical Hacking and Analysis

Ethical hacking and security analysis are at the forefront of protecting organizations from cyber threats. While hackers are often viewed negatively, **ethical hackers**, or **white-hat hackers**, play a critical role in identifying vulnerabilities before malicious hackers can exploit them.

1. **Penetration                          Testing**
   Ethical hackers use techniques similar to those of malicious hackers to **penetrate systems** and identify weaknesses. By conducting **penetration tests**, ethical hackers help organizations understand their vulnerabilities and take proactive measures to secure their networks and data.

2. **Vulnerability Assessments and Threat Analysis**
   Security analysts use a variety of tools and

techniques to conduct **vulnerability assessments** and **threat analysis**. By continuously monitoring networks for suspicious activity and identifying potential risks, analysts ensure that organizations are prepared to respond quickly to potential attacks.

3. **Legal and Ethical Responsibilities** Ethical hackers must follow legal and ethical guidelines when testing systems. They must obtain permission before attempting to breach systems and always act in the best interests of the organizations they are protecting. This professional responsibility makes ethical hacking an indispensable part of modern cybersecurity.

---

## Conclusion: The Vital Role of Cybersecurity in the Modern World

Cybersecurity is no longer a niche field—it's a cornerstone of modern business, government, and personal safety. The increasing frequency and complexity of cyberattacks highlight the need for skilled cybersecurity professionals who can protect digital assets from malicious actors. As we continue to digitize nearly every aspect of life, the demand

27

for cybersecurity talent will only increase, making it one of the most exciting and rewarding career paths in tech today.

In the next chapters, we will delve into the **specific roles** within the cybersecurity industry, the **skills required** to succeed, and how you can embark on a career in cybersecurity, whether as an ethical hacker, security analyst, or beyond.

---

This chapter provides an in-depth look at the cybersecurity landscape, the importance of protecting digital assets, and how the role of cybersecurity professionals is more crucial than ever in today's world. Let me know if you'd like to adjust or expand on any part of it!

# CHAPTER 2

# THE RISE OF CYBERSECURITY THREATS

**Understanding Common Threats: Malware, Ransomware, Phishing, and More**

Cybersecurity threats have become more sophisticated and widespread in recent years, and understanding the different types of threats is essential for both businesses and individuals looking to protect their digital assets. These threats range from malicious software programs to social engineering attacks aimed at exploiting human behavior. Let's break down some of the most common types of cyber threats that organizations and individuals face today:

1. **Malware**

   Malware is short for **malicious software** and refers to any software specifically designed to cause damage to a computer, server, or network. Malware can take many forms, including:

- o **Viruses**: Programs that attach themselves to legitimate files or programs and spread to other systems.
- o **Worms**: Self-replicating programs that spread over networks, often exploiting vulnerabilities in operating systems.
- o **Trojans**: Malicious software disguised as legitimate software that tricks users into installing it, allowing hackers to gain access to systems.
- o **Spyware**: Software that secretly monitors a user's activity, often collecting sensitive data such as login credentials or personal information.
- o **Adware**: Unwanted software that automatically displays ads, often at the cost of system performance or user privacy.

2. **Ransomware**

Ransomware is a type of malware that encrypts the victim's files or locks them out of their system, demanding a ransom in exchange for restoring access. This type of attack has become increasingly common and can cause significant disruption for both individuals and businesses. Victims are often threatened with the permanent loss of their data if they do not comply with the ransom demands.

3. **Phishing**

    Phishing is a form of **social engineering** where attackers use fraudulent emails, websites, or messages to trick individuals into revealing sensitive information, such as passwords, credit card details, or personal identification numbers (PINs). Phishing attacks can be highly convincing, often impersonating legitimate organizations like banks, social media platforms, or government entities.

4. **Denial-of-Service (DoS) and Distributed Denial-of-Service (DDoS)**

    DoS and DDoS attacks are designed to overwhelm a network or website with traffic, rendering it unavailable to users. While a DoS attack comes from a single source, a DDoS attack uses multiple systems (often hijacked devices in a **botnet**) to flood the target system with traffic, making it even more difficult to mitigate.

5. **SQL Injection**

    SQL injection attacks exploit vulnerabilities in a website or application that uses **SQL databases**. Attackers can insert malicious code into an SQL query, giving them unauthorized access to a system's database and potentially allowing them to view, modify, or delete data.

---

**Examples of Large-Scale Cyberattacks**

Cyberattacks have become an ongoing threat to organizations, individuals, and even entire nations. Below are some examples of high-profile cyberattacks that demonstrate the far-reaching consequences of these threats:

1. **The WannaCry Ransomware Attack (2017)**
   In May 2017, the **WannaCry ransomware** attack affected hundreds of thousands of computers across 150 countries. The attack exploited a vulnerability in the **Microsoft Windows operating system**, which had been discovered by the **National Security Agency (NSA)** but was leaked by a hacker group known as **Shadow Brokers**. Once the vulnerability was exploited, the ransomware encrypted files and demanded a ransom of $300 in Bitcoin.

   The attack caused widespread disruption, including halting operations at **the UK's National Health**

**Service (NHS)**, where hospitals were forced to cancel appointments and turn away patients. The attack also affected major corporations, including **FedEx** and **Nissan**. The WannaCry ransomware attack highlighted the importance of regular software updates and patch management to prevent vulnerabilities from being exploited.

2. **The Equifax Data Breach (2017)**
   In September 2017, the **Equifax data breach** exposed the personal information of **143 million Americans**. The breach occurred when cybercriminals exploited a known vulnerability in the **Apache Struts** web application framework. The attackers gained access to sensitive data, including social security numbers, birth dates, and credit card information.

   The breach had widespread consequences, with affected individuals at risk of **identity theft** and **fraud**. Equifax faced legal action, fines, and a significant loss of consumer trust. The breach emphasized the importance of strong cybersecurity measures, timely software patching, and effective data protection protocols.

3. **The SolarWinds Hack (2020)**
The **SolarWinds hack**, discovered in late 2020, was a sophisticated cyber espionage attack that compromised the systems of **U.S. government agencies**, including the **Department of Homeland Security** and the **Treasury Department**. The attackers, believed to be state-sponsored, infiltrated the **SolarWinds Orion** software, which was used by thousands of organizations worldwide for network monitoring.

The attack allowed hackers to monitor and potentially manipulate communications within these agencies for several months before being detected. The SolarWinds hack demonstrated the vulnerabilities in widely used software and the risks of supply chain attacks, where trusted third-party vendors are targeted to gain access to organizations' systems.

**How Cyber Threats Have Evolved Over Time**

Cyber threats have evolved significantly over the past few decades, becoming more sophisticated, targeted, and pervasive. Here's a brief look at how these threats have developed over time:

1. **The Early Days: Viruses and Worms**
   In the early days of cybersecurity, attacks were often simple **viruses** and **worms** designed to spread from one computer to another, causing disruptions like system crashes or slowdowns. These attacks were often seen as a nuisance, though they could cause significant damage to individual users or organizations.

2. **The Rise of Ransomware and Advanced Malware**
   As the internet grew and businesses became more dependent on digital infrastructure, cybercriminals began developing more sophisticated forms of malware, such as **ransomware**. Rather than just disrupting systems, ransomware attacks could hold valuable data hostage, demanding payment in exchange for restoring access. These types of attacks became more financially motivated, with

cybercriminals targeting businesses, governments, and individuals alike.

3.  **Targeted Attacks and Nation-State Cyberwarfare**
    Over the past decade, cyberattacks have become more **targeted** and **state-sponsored**, with cybercriminals and even nation-states using digital tools for espionage, data theft, and even disruption of critical infrastructure. Cyber warfare is now a recognized part of geopolitical conflict, with state actors using **cyberattacks** as a tool for espionage and destabilization, as seen in incidents like the **Stuxnet virus** and **the SolarWinds hack**.

4.  **Social Engineering and Phishing**
    As technology advanced, so did the methods used by attackers. **Social engineering**—the manipulation of individuals into divulging confidential information—became a powerful tool for cybercriminals. Phishing attacks, where hackers impersonate legitimate organizations to trick individuals into sharing personal information or login credentials, have become one of the most common cyber threats today.

**The Global Impact of Cybercrime on Economies and Businesses**

Cybercrime is not just a local problem; it has a profound global impact on economies, businesses, and governments. According to the **Cybersecurity Ventures 2020 Report**, cybercrime is projected to cost the world **$10.5 trillion annually** by 2025, up from **$3 trillion** in 2015. This alarming increase is driven by several factors:

1. **Financial                                        Losses**

   The financial impact of cyberattacks on businesses is staggering. In addition to the direct costs of the attack (such as ransomware payments and remediation costs), businesses also face long-term expenses such as reputational damage, legal fees, and regulatory fines. **Small businesses** are particularly vulnerable, with many lacking the resources to defend against sophisticated cyber threats.

2. **Disruption               to               Operations**

   Cyberattacks can disrupt critical business operations, leading to downtime, loss of productivity, and delays in product or service delivery. For example, a **DDoS attack** can render a website or service inaccessible for hours or days, causing a loss of revenue and customer trust. Ransomware attacks can lock organizations out of their own systems, preventing them from conducting business as usual.

3. **Impact on National Security and Critical Infrastructure**

   Cybercrime also affects national security and critical infrastructure. Attacks on energy grids, transportation systems, and healthcare facilities can have far-reaching consequences, impacting millions of lives. For instance, cyberattacks targeting hospitals during the **COVID-19 pandemic** disrupted medical services, putting patients' lives at risk.

4. **Increased Costs for Businesses and Governments**

   To defend against the growing threat of cybercrime, businesses and governments must invest heavily in cybersecurity measures. This includes deploying security tools, hiring skilled cybersecurity professionals, and conducting regular security audits. The ongoing cost of cybersecurity investments is a significant burden for organizations, particularly smaller companies that may struggle to afford comprehensive security solutions.

## Conclusion: Understanding the Growing Cybersecurity Threat Landscape

The rise of cybersecurity threats has brought about a new era of digital warfare, where malicious actors are targeting organizations, governments, and individuals with increasingly sophisticated tactics. As cyber threats continue to evolve, so too must our defense mechanisms. Understanding the types of threats, the evolution of cybercrime, and the global impact of these attacks is crucial for both cybersecurity professionals and the general public.

As we progress through this book, we will explore how to protect yourself and your organization from these threats, what tools and strategies can be used to defend against cyberattacks, and how ethical hacking and analysis play a crucial role in combating cybercrime.

---

This chapter provides an in-depth look at the various cybersecurity threats, offering real-world examples of major attacks and their impact on businesses, individuals, and economies. Let me know if you'd like to explore any specific details further or add additional examples!

# CHAPTER 3

# DIFFERENT ROLES IN CYBERSECURITY

## Overview of the Cybersecurity Career Path

Cybersecurity is a dynamic and rapidly growing field, offering numerous career paths for individuals with diverse skill sets. Whether you're just starting out in tech or looking to make a career change, there are multiple entry points and roles to explore in cybersecurity. The growing prevalence of cyber threats and the increasing complexity of digital infrastructures mean that skilled professionals are in high demand. From hands-on technical roles to management and consulting positions, the field offers a broad range of opportunities.

The career path in cybersecurity typically begins with foundational knowledge of computer networks, security protocols, and systems administration. As professionals gain experience, they can specialize in various aspects of cybersecurity, from ethical hacking and incident response to threat analysis and risk management. Many cybersecurity roles require specific skills, certifications, and an understanding of both the technical and strategic aspects of security.

In this chapter, we will explore the most common roles in cybersecurity, outline the skills required for each, and provide real-life examples of professionals in these roles. We will also discuss how to choose the right role based on your interests and skill set.

---

**Differentiating Between Roles: Ethical Hacker, Security Analyst, Penetration Tester, SOC Analyst, and More**

1. **Ethical                                        Hacker**

   An **ethical hacker**—also known as a **white-hat hacker**—uses hacking techniques to identify vulnerabilities in a system, network, or application, but does so legally and with permission from the organization. The goal is to find weaknesses before malicious hackers can exploit them. Ethical hackers may perform tasks such as vulnerability assessments, penetration tests, and security audits.

   **Key Responsibilities**:

o Conduct penetration tests to identify vulnerabilities.

o Report findings and recommend remediation measures.

o Use hacking tools to simulate attacks and identify weak points in an organization's security.

o Work with development teams to improve security features.

**Real-life                                         Example**:
**Katie Moussouris**, a well-known ethical hacker, worked with **Microsoft** to develop their bug bounty programs and improve security. Her work in identifying vulnerabilities has helped improve security at major tech firms.

2. **Security                                         Analyst**
A **security analyst** is responsible for protecting an organization's computer systems and networks from cyber threats. They monitor network traffic, identify potential vulnerabilities, and investigate security breaches. Security analysts often work within an organization's **Security Operations Center (SOC)**

and use a variety of tools to detect and respond to security incidents.

**Key Responsibilities**:

- o Monitor network traffic and system activity for signs of suspicious behavior.
- o Respond to and investigate security incidents and breaches.
- o Implement and maintain security software, such as firewalls, antivirus programs, and encryption tools.
- o Conduct regular security audits and assessments.

**Real-life** **Example**:
**Carlos Perez**, a security analyst, worked for **Tenable**, a leading cybersecurity company, where he developed tools for vulnerability management. His role involved identifying weaknesses in both internal systems and external-facing platforms.

3. **Penetration Tester (Pen Tester)**
A **penetration tester** (often called a **pen tester**) simulates cyberattacks on an organization's systems,

applications, and networks to identify security weaknesses before malicious actors can exploit them. While similar to ethical hackers, pen testers are more specialized in testing systems for vulnerabilities that could be exploited by real-world attackers.

**Key Responsibilities**:

- o Conduct comprehensive penetration tests on systems, applications, and networks.
- o Report vulnerabilities and provide recommendations for fixing them.
- o Stay up-to-date on new tools, techniques, and vulnerabilities in the hacking community.
- o Collaborate with development and IT teams to remediate vulnerabilities.

**Real-life** **Example**: **Timothy Goh**, a penetration tester at **Synopsys**, specializes in performing penetration tests for clients in sectors such as healthcare, finance, and technology. His work helps organizations secure critical systems and improve their overall security posture.

4. **Security Operations Center (SOC) Analyst**
   SOC analysts work in the **Security Operations Center**, where they monitor and respond to security threats in real-time. They use a combination of tools and techniques to detect, analyze, and respond to potential incidents, often acting as the first line of defense against cyberattacks. SOC analysts work in shifts to ensure 24/7 coverage of security operations.

**Key Responsibilities**:

- o Monitor security systems and logs for signs of intrusion or suspicious activity.
- o Analyze alerts generated by security monitoring tools (such as SIEM platforms).
- o Investigate incidents and escalate them to higher-level analysts or incident response teams as needed.
- o Maintain and update security protocols and documentation.

**Real-life**                              **Example**:
**Michael L. Wilson**, a SOC analyst at **SonicWall**, works to monitor network and system activities for signs of malicious activity. He uses advanced SIEM

tools to analyze incidents and ensure the organization is protected against emerging threats.

## 5. Incident                                    Responder

**Incident responders** are responsible for managing and mitigating the aftermath of a cyberattack or security breach. They lead efforts to identify the source of the attack, assess the damage, and restore systems and data. Incident responders play a crucial role in minimizing the impact of cyber incidents and preventing future breaches.

**Key Responsibilities**:

- o Respond to and manage cybersecurity incidents and breaches.
- o Conduct root cause analysis to determine how the attack occurred.
- o Work with forensic teams to collect evidence and track the attacker's movements.
- o Implement corrective actions to prevent similar incidents in the future.

**Real-life                                    Example**:

**Chris Wysopal**, a former hacker and current

**Veracode** co-founder, has worked as an incident responder during various large-scale security breaches. His expertise in understanding how hackers think allows him to build stronger security defenses and respond effectively to incidents.

6. **Chief Information Security Officer (CISO)**
The **CISO** is the highest-ranking security officer within an organization, responsible for overseeing the organization's cybersecurity strategy. They manage the entire security team, develop policies and protocols, and ensure the organization complies with legal and regulatory requirements related to security.

**Key Responsibilities**:

- o Develop and implement a company-wide cybersecurity strategy.
- o Manage security staff and provide leadership on cybersecurity initiatives.
- o Ensure compliance with industry standards and regulations (e.g., GDPR, HIPAA).
- o Work with executive teams to align cybersecurity initiatives with business goals.

**Real-life** **Example**: **Ruth McCauley**, a CISO at **GE Healthcare**, has been responsible for building and overseeing a comprehensive cybersecurity program that protects patient data and ensures compliance with healthcare regulations like **HIPAA**.

---

## How to Choose the Right Role Based on Your Interests and Skills

With a wide range of roles in cybersecurity, it's essential to align your interests and strengths with the job that best fits you. Here's how to decide:

1. **If you enjoy problem-solving and ethical challenges**:
   Consider becoming an **ethical hacker** or a **penetration tester**. These roles require a keen interest in discovering vulnerabilities and understanding the tactics used by malicious hackers. You'll need strong technical skills and an inquisitive mindset.

2. **If you are detail-oriented and enjoy monitoring systems**:

   A role as a **security analyst** or **SOC analyst** might be a good fit. These positions require individuals who can spot patterns, detect anomalies, and respond swiftly to security incidents.

3. **If you're interested in leadership and strategy**:
   A career as a **CISO** or a cybersecurity manager could be a great option. These roles involve overseeing security operations, developing policies, and ensuring the entire organization is protected.

4. **If you like to investigate and analyze security breaches**:

   **Incident response** roles require individuals who are calm under pressure, analytical, and able to work efficiently to contain and mitigate attacks.

5. **If you prefer working with teams to implement security                          measures**:

   **Security engineers** or **risk management** roles may suit you if you like working with teams to set up systems and protocols that proactively secure infrastructure and mitigate risks.

**Conclusion**

The field of cybersecurity offers a wide range of career paths, each with unique responsibilities and opportunities. Whether you are drawn to technical, analytical, or leadership roles, there is a place for you in the cybersecurity workforce. By understanding the various roles and the skills required for each, you can make an informed decision about which path to pursue. As the demand for cybersecurity professionals continues to grow, there will be numerous opportunities for you to make a meaningful impact in protecting our digital world.

---

This chapter provides an in-depth look at the different career roles within cybersecurity, offering real-world examples and practical advice on how to choose the right role based on your skills and interests. Let me know if you'd like more details on any specific role or examples!

# CHAPTER 4

# BASIC SKILLS EVERY CYBERSECURITY PROFESSIONAL NEEDS

**Introduction: The Foundation of a Cybersecurity Career**

Cybersecurity is a multifaceted field that requires both **technical** and **soft skills**. While technical expertise is crucial for understanding how to protect networks, systems, and applications, soft skills play an equally important role in navigating the complexities of security challenges, collaborating with teams, and effectively communicating security issues to non-technical stakeholders. This chapter will break down the core skills needed for a successful career in cybersecurity, highlighting both **technical** and **soft skills** and providing real-world examples of how these skills are applied in the industry.

**Core Technical Skills: Networking, Operating Systems, and Protocols**

1. **Networking Basics**

**Networking** is the backbone of cybersecurity. A solid understanding of networking fundamentals is critical for anyone working in cybersecurity. Networks are how data flows between devices, and understanding how networks function enables you to recognize vulnerabilities and secure data transmission.

**Key Areas to Understand**:

- o **TCP/IP Stack**: The Transmission Control Protocol/Internet Protocol (TCP/IP) is the suite of communication protocols used for transmitting data over a network. Familiarity with **IP addressing, subnetting, DNS**, and **DHCP** is crucial for network security.
- o **Routers and Switches**: Understanding how these devices manage data traffic and their role in network security, such as how firewalls and intrusion detection systems (IDS) are configured to protect against unauthorized access.

   o  **Firewall Configuration**: Firewalls are used to block unauthorized access and monitor incoming and outgoing traffic. A cybersecurity professional must know how to configure firewalls and VPNs to protect a network.

**Real-World**                    **Example**: **John**, a network security administrator at a financial institution, monitors network traffic using **Wireshark** to detect unusual patterns indicative of a **DDoS attack**. His deep understanding of **IP protocols** and **traffic routing** enables him to identify and mitigate the attack before it disrupts operations.

2. **Operating Systems**

Cybersecurity professionals must have a solid grasp of various **operating systems**, particularly those used in enterprise environments, including **Windows**, **Linux**, and **macOS**. Each operating system has its own vulnerabilities, security features, and methods for defending against attacks.

**Key Areas to Understand**:

- o **System Hardening**: The process of securing a system by reducing its surface of vulnerability. For example, disabling unnecessary services or patching known vulnerabilities in operating systems.

- o **Access Control**: Understanding user permissions, user rights, and authentication methods to prevent unauthorized access to critical systems.

- o **File Systems**: Understanding how data is stored, managed, and encrypted on operating systems, as attackers often exploit weaknesses in file systems to steal or corrupt data.

**Real-World                                    Example**:
**Sarah**, a system administrator at a tech company, conducts regular **patch management** for her organization's **Linux servers**. She applies security patches as soon as they are released, minimizing the risk of exploitation from known vulnerabilities. Sarah's in-depth knowledge of **Linux file systems** ensures she can detect any unusual activity indicating a possible breach.

3. **Protocols**

**Protocols** are rules that govern data communication between devices. Understanding how different protocols work is essential for securing communication and preventing attacks that target protocol weaknesses.

**Key Protocols to Understand**:

- **HTTP/HTTPS**: Hypertext Transfer Protocol (HTTP) is used for web communication. HTTPS, the secure version, encrypts data to protect user privacy.
- **SMTP/POP3/IMAP**: These protocols are used for email communication. Understanding how email protocols work helps protect against email-based threats like **phishing** and **email spoofing**.
- **FTP/SFTP**: File Transfer Protocol (FTP) and Secure FTP (SFTP) are used to transfer files. It's essential to understand how these protocols work and how to secure them to prevent unauthorized data transfers.

**Real-World** **Example**: **Luis**, a penetration tester, used his knowledge of **HTTP** and **SSL/TLS protocols** to identify and exploit vulnerabilities in a company's web application during a security audit. He demonstrated how **HTTP traffic** could be intercepted and manipulated if **SSL/TLS** encryption was not properly configured, leading to a vulnerability that could compromise sensitive data.

---

**Soft Skills: Problem-Solving, Attention to Detail, and Communication**

While technical expertise is essential, soft skills are just as important in a cybersecurity career. In a field where threats evolve constantly, the ability to think critically and solve problems is vital. Similarly, attention to detail and clear communication help cybersecurity professionals effectively manage security issues, explain findings to stakeholders, and work collaboratively with teams.

1. **Problem-Solving**

Cybersecurity often requires quick thinking and creative solutions, especially when dealing with a new or unknown attack. Cybersecurity professionals must approach problems methodically, diagnosing the source of security incidents and crafting effective solutions under pressure.

**Key Problem-Solving Skills**:

- o **Incident Investigation**: The ability to trace the source of a security breach or vulnerability.
- o **Mitigation Strategies**: Finding ways to stop attacks in progress and prevent future occurrences.
- o **Forensic Analysis**: Using data to analyze cyberattacks, determine how they happened, and gather evidence for legal or compliance purposes.

**Real-World** **Example**:
**Maria**, a cybersecurity analyst, is faced with a **phishing** attack that has breached her organization's email system. Using her problem-solving skills, Maria analyzes the email headers to trace the attack's

origin, isolates the compromised accounts, and implements additional security protocols to prevent future incidents.

2. **Attention to Detail**

In cybersecurity, small oversights can lead to large-scale breaches. Attention to detail is critical when reviewing logs, analyzing network traffic, or identifying anomalies in system performance. Cybersecurity professionals must meticulously inspect systems, search for hidden threats, and recognize the subtleties of potential attacks.

**Key Attention-to-Detail Tasks**:

- o **Log Analysis**: Reviewing system logs for signs of suspicious activity.
- o **Vulnerability Assessment**: Conducting detailed scans to uncover overlooked weaknesses.
- o **Monitoring Traffic**: Watching for unusual traffic patterns that may indicate an attack.

**Real-World                                          Example**:
**Ethan**, a SOC analyst, was reviewing network traffic

58

and noticed an unusual spike in data sent from an internal server to an external IP address. His attention to detail led him to uncover a **data exfiltration attempt**, where sensitive customer data was being transferred without authorization. He immediately flagged the activity and stopped the attack.

## 3. Communication

Strong communication skills are essential for cybersecurity professionals, as they often need to explain complex technical issues to non-technical colleagues, customers, and stakeholders. Additionally, cybersecurity professionals must be able to communicate clearly and effectively during incidents, helping teams coordinate responses and ensuring everyone is on the same page.

**Key Communication Skills**:

- o **Incident Reporting**: Writing clear, concise reports during or after an incident.
- o **Explaining Security Risks**: Communicating security risks and mitigation strategies to non-technical decision-makers.

o **Collaborating with Teams**: Coordinating with other IT and security team members during incidents and projects.

**Real-World                    Example**: **Tasha**, a CISO (Chief Information Security Officer), was tasked with explaining the importance of a new security policy to the board of directors at her company. Using her communication skills, she was able to translate the technical details of the policy into terms that the board understood, ultimately securing their approval for a company-wide implementation.

## Conclusion

In the rapidly evolving field of cybersecurity, a successful professional needs a combination of **core technical skills** and **soft skills** to adapt and respond to emerging threats. Technical expertise in networking, operating systems, protocols, and tools is critical for securing systems and networks. At the same time, soft skills such as problem-solving, attention to detail, and communication enable cybersecurity professionals to tackle complex challenges and effectively work with teams and stakeholders.

As you progress in your cybersecurity career, these skills will serve as the foundation for your success. In the next chapters, we will delve into specific tools and techniques that cybersecurity professionals use in their day-to-day roles, building on the skills covered in this chapter to give you a complete understanding of how to navigate this dynamic and rewarding field.

---

This chapter highlights the essential skills needed to start and succeed in a cybersecurity career, combining both technical knowledge and soft skills.

# CHAPTER 5

# *GETTING STARTED IN CYBERSECURITY*

## Introduction: Breaking Into Cybersecurity Without Prior Experience

The world of cybersecurity is vast, dynamic, and full of opportunities. As organizations across the globe struggle to protect themselves from the increasing number of cyber threats, the demand for skilled cybersecurity professionals continues to grow. The good news is that breaking into cybersecurity is entirely possible, even if you don't have a technical background. The field is open to people from all walks of life, and with the right approach, you can transition into a rewarding career in cybersecurity.

This chapter will guide you on how to get started in cybersecurity without prior experience, highlighting key learning resources, certifications, and real-world case studies of individuals who made the successful transition into the field.

**How to Break into Cybersecurity with No Prior Experience**

Starting a career in cybersecurity without experience may seem daunting, but it's far more achievable than it may appear. Here's a step-by-step guide on how to break into the field:

1. **Start with the Basics**
   Before diving into advanced cybersecurity topics, it's essential to get a solid understanding of **basic IT concepts**. Start by learning about computer systems, operating systems (especially **Linux** and **Windows**), networking fundamentals (e.g., TCP/IP, subnets, DNS), and security principles. A strong foundation in IT will make it easier to understand more advanced topics in cybersecurity later on.

   **Actionable Tip:**
   Spend time getting familiar with **command-line interfaces (CLI)**, as many cybersecurity tools rely on terminal commands, especially in environments like **Linux**.

63

2. **Enroll in Online Courses**

There are numerous online platforms that offer beginner-friendly courses specifically tailored to those new to cybersecurity. These courses cover everything from networking basics to ethical hacking and incident response. Many platforms also provide hands-on labs where you can practice what you've learned.

**Recommended Platforms**:

- o **Coursera**: Offers a range of cybersecurity courses, including **Google IT Support Professional Certificate** and **IBM Cybersecurity Analyst Professional Certificate**.
- o **Udemy**: Features various affordable courses such as **Cyber Security for Beginners** and **The Complete Cyber Security Course** by Nathan House.
- o **edX**: Offers courses in partnership with top universities, such as **Introduction to Cyber Security** by **NYU Tandon School of Engineering**.

o **Cybrary**: Offers free courses on cybersecurity fundamentals and more advanced topics like penetration testing and malware analysis.

3. **Practice with Virtual Labs**

Once you have a basic understanding, it's time to get hands-on experience. Virtual labs are environments that allow you to practice penetration testing, network defense, and other cybersecurity activities in a controlled, simulated environment. These labs let you experiment without the risk of damaging any real systems.

**Recommended Lab Platforms**:

o **TryHackMe**: A gamified platform that helps beginners learn cybersecurity concepts through guided challenges and hands-on labs.

o **Hack The Box**: Offers a variety of challenges where you can practice ethical hacking techniques on real-world scenarios.

o **OverTheWire**: Provides a collection of online war games for cybersecurity practice, with a focus on Linux-based systems and ethical hacking.

4. **Start with Entry-Level Roles**

You don't need to jump straight into a cybersecurity analyst or ethical hacker role. Start with entry-level positions in IT or networking, such as a **Help Desk Technician** or **System Administrator**, which will give you exposure to the types of systems and networks you'll later be protecting. Many cybersecurity professionals start their careers in these roles and gradually transition into more specialized cybersecurity positions.

**Actionable** **Tip**:
Look for **internships**, **volunteer positions**, or **freelance opportunities** where you can practice cybersecurity in real-world settings, even if it's on a smaller scale.

---

## Learning Resources: Online Courses, Certifications, and Boot Camps

1. **Online Courses**

Online courses are a fantastic way to learn at your own pace. Many well-known platforms offer **free** or

**affordable** courses that cover everything from basic IT knowledge to advanced cybersecurity skills. Some of these courses offer certifications upon completion, which can help build your resume.

**Example**:

The **Google IT Support Professional Certificate** on Coursera is a great starting point for those with no technical background. It teaches fundamental IT skills that will serve as a foundation for more advanced cybersecurity topics.

2. **Certifications**

Cybersecurity certifications are a key component of breaking into the field, as they provide a recognized benchmark for your knowledge and skills. The right certifications can make you stand out to potential employers.

**Recommended Entry-Level Certifications**:

- o **CompTIA IT Fundamentals (ITF+)**: A beginner-friendly certification that introduces basic IT concepts and prepares you for more advanced certifications.

- **CompTIA Security+**: A foundational certification covering cybersecurity principles, threats, and vulnerabilities. It's highly recognized in the industry as a starting point for cybersecurity professionals.
- **Certified Ethical Hacker (CEH)**: For those who wish to pursue a career in ethical hacking, the CEH certification provides knowledge of hacking tools and techniques used by cybersecurity professionals.
- **Cisco Certified CyberOps Associate**: An entry-level certification that provides an understanding of cybersecurity operations, particularly for roles in Security Operations Centers (SOC).

3. **Boot                                                        Camps**

Cybersecurity boot camps are immersive, short-term training programs designed to equip you with hands-on skills in a condensed timeframe. These boot camps often focus on practical, real-world skills and are typically geared towards people making a career change.

**Recommended Boot Camps**:

- o **Flatiron School**: Offers a **Cybersecurity Engineering** boot camp that covers the foundational skills needed for entry-level cybersecurity positions.
- o **Springboard**: Offers a **Cybersecurity Career Track** that guarantees job placement within six months of completion.
- o **Cybersecurity Bootcamp by University of California, Berkeley**: This program covers all aspects of cybersecurity, including penetration testing, risk management, and ethical hacking.

**Real-World Case Studies: Individuals Who Transitioned into Cybersecurity from Non-Tech Roles**

1. **Sarah's Journey: From Healthcare to Cybersecurity Analyst**
   Sarah had worked as a **nurse** for over a decade, but her interest in technology and problem-solving led her to make a career change. She started by taking online courses in IT fundamentals, followed by the **CompTIA Security+** certification. She then

transitioned to a **Security Analyst** role at a healthcare company. By leveraging her previous healthcare experience, she was able to apply her new technical skills to protect sensitive patient data and meet industry compliance regulations. Sarah now works as a cybersecurity consultant, helping healthcare organizations strengthen their defenses against cyber threats.

2. **James' Journey: From Retail Management to Penetration Tester**

James was a **retail manager** with little to no experience in technology but had always been interested in computers and security. After discovering ethical hacking, he took a **web development boot camp** and self-studied cybersecurity topics in his free time. He then pursued the **Certified Ethical Hacker (CEH)** certification. Today, James works as a **penetration tester**, helping companies test their security by exploiting vulnerabilities in their systems before cybercriminals can. His attention to detail and analytical skills from his retail management days helped him excel in identifying weaknesses in networks and applications.

3. **Emma's Journey: From Customer Service to Cybersecurity                    Consultant**

Emma had worked in **customer service** for years, but her growing interest in online security led her to take the leap into cybersecurity. After completing the **Google IT Support Certificate** and earning the **CompTIA Security+ certification**, Emma landed an internship with a cybersecurity firm. Within a year, she was promoted to a **cybersecurity consultant**, helping clients identify security gaps and implement robust defenses. Emma's ability to communicate complex technical issues in a clear and accessible way made her a valuable asset to clients who needed help understanding their cybersecurity needs.

## Conclusion

Breaking into cybersecurity with no prior experience may seem challenging, but it is entirely achievable with the right mindset, resources, and dedication. By starting with foundational IT knowledge, leveraging online courses and certifications, and gaining hands-on experience through labs

71

or entry-level positions, anyone can successfully transition into this fast-growing and rewarding field.

In the next chapters, we will dive deeper into specific cybersecurity roles and the skills needed to excel in them, offering you a roadmap to pursue your desired career in cybersecurity.

---

This chapter provides actionable steps for getting started in cybersecurity, including learning resources, certifications, and real-world case studies of individuals who successfully transitioned into the field.

# CHAPTER 6

# UNDERSTANDING ETHICAL HACKING

## Introduction: What Is Ethical Hacking?

Ethical hacking, also known as **white-hat hacking**, is the practice of intentionally probing computer systems, networks, and applications for vulnerabilities to identify weaknesses that could be exploited by malicious hackers. Ethical hackers use the same tools, techniques, and methods as cybercriminals but do so with the permission of the organization in order to help protect against cyberattacks. These professionals are often called **penetration testers**, **security auditors**, or **red teamers**, and they play a critical role in the overall cybersecurity strategy of organizations.

The goal of ethical hacking is not to exploit vulnerabilities for personal gain, but to discover weaknesses before malicious hackers (black-hat hackers) can use them for criminal activities. Ethical hackers help strengthen security defenses, protect sensitive data, and ensure that systems remain resilient in the face of potential attacks. As cyber threats continue to evolve, the role of ethical hackers has become more crucial in safeguarding digital infrastructures.

---

**The Role of Ethical Hacking in Cybersecurity**

Ethical hacking plays an essential role in preventing data breaches, protecting intellectual property, and ensuring the smooth functioning of critical infrastructures. Here's how ethical hackers contribute to the cybersecurity landscape:

1. **Identifying Vulnerabilities Before Malicious Hackers Can Exploit Them**
   Ethical hackers use a variety of tools and techniques to simulate real-world attacks, probing for weaknesses such as software flaws, misconfigurations, and insecure network protocols. By finding these vulnerabilities, ethical hackers help organizations address issues before cybercriminals can take advantage of them.

2. **Conducting Penetration Tests (Pen Tests)**
   Penetration testing is a primary activity for ethical hackers, where they conduct controlled tests on systems and networks to simulate a breach. The

findings from these tests help organizations understand their security posture and make improvements. Pen testing often includes **network security assessments**, **web application testing**, and **social engineering simulations** (e.g., phishing).

3. **Strengthening        Security        Protocols**
   By identifying potential attack vectors, ethical hackers assist organizations in strengthening their security protocols. This includes improving **encryption standards**, enhancing **authentication mechanisms**, and ensuring **firewall configurations** are properly implemented.

4. **Security        Audits        and        Compliance**
   Ethical hackers help companies stay compliant with industry standards and regulations such as **GDPR**, **HIPAA**, and **PCI DSS**. Many regulatory frameworks require organizations to conduct regular security audits and address any vulnerabilities that could compromise the privacy of data or the security of systems.

5. **Creating    a    Proactive    Security    Culture**
   Ethical hackers contribute to the development of a proactive security culture within organizations. By identifying security gaps and recommending

improvements, they raise awareness of cybersecurity risks, ensuring that all team members are engaged in the effort to secure systems.

---

**Real-World Examples of Ethical Hackers Identifying Vulnerabilities in Companies**

1. **The Tesla Bug Bounty Program**
   In 2014, **Tesla** launched a **bug bounty program** to encourage ethical hackers to identify vulnerabilities in their vehicle systems and internal infrastructure. This program rewarded ethical hackers for finding flaws in Tesla's systems, which could be used to exploit the vehicles' software or break into internal networks.

   In 2019, ethical hacker **Qihoo 360** discovered a vulnerability in Tesla's **in-vehicle infotainment system** that could allow an attacker to remotely control the car's navigation system. Tesla responded quickly by patching the vulnerability, demonstrating how ethical hacking can play a key role in protecting IoT devices such as self-driving cars.

**Real-World Impact**: Tesla's bug bounty program helped identify and fix critical vulnerabilities before they could be exploited by malicious hackers, preventing potential cyberattacks on their vehicles and ensuring user safety.

2. **The Facebook Bug Bounty Program**
Facebook's **bug bounty program** invites ethical hackers to find and report vulnerabilities in its platforms. In 2018, **Ashraf Taha**, a security researcher, discovered a vulnerability in Facebook's **"view as"** feature, which allowed attackers to steal users' access tokens and potentially hijack their accounts.

Facebook rewarded Taha with a **$40,000** bounty for identifying the flaw. The vulnerability was swiftly patched, preventing hackers from exploiting it to access private user data. This example highlights the importance of ethical hackers in protecting user privacy and securing online platforms.

**Real-World Impact**: Facebook's proactive approach in working with ethical hackers ensures that they can maintain a secure platform, minimizing the risk of user data being compromised.

3. **The 2017 Equifax Data Breach**
Although the **Equifax breach** was a massive failure in cybersecurity, it provides a case for the importance of ethical hacking in identifying and patching vulnerabilities. The breach, which exposed the personal data of over **143 million people**, was caused by an unpatched vulnerability in the **Apache Struts** framework used by Equifax.

Ethical hackers could have potentially discovered and reported the vulnerability before it was exploited by attackers. This breach underlined the necessity of regularly testing systems for vulnerabilities, patching software promptly, and maintaining a strong relationship with ethical hackers and security professionals to avoid such incidents.

**Real-World Impact**: The breach served as a wake-up call to organizations about the consequences of neglecting proactive security measures and the value of having ethical hackers test systems regularly to identify weaknesses.

## The Ethical Dilemma of Hacking: Understanding the Boundaries

While ethical hacking plays a vital role in cybersecurity, it also comes with a set of ethical dilemmas that require careful consideration. The line between ethical hacking and malicious hacking is thin, and understanding the boundaries is crucial for ethical hackers to avoid crossing into illegal activity.

1. **Obtaining                              Permission**

   Ethical hackers can only test systems and networks if they have explicit permission from the organization. Unauthorized hacking, even if intended to be beneficial, is illegal and can result in criminal charges. This highlights the importance of clearly defined contracts and written agreements between ethical hackers and the organizations they are hired by.

2. **The          Scope          of          Engagement**

   Ethical hackers must also understand the scope of their engagement. Their activities should be confined to the areas specified in their contracts. Overstepping the agreed-upon boundaries can result in unintended consequences, such as compromising sensitive information or disrupting business operations. Ethical hackers must ensure that their testing is limited to the systems that were authorized.

3. **Disclosure of Vulnerabilities**
   When ethical hackers discover vulnerabilities, they are responsible for reporting them in a way that minimizes the risk of exploitation. The ethical dilemma arises when deciding how much information to disclose. For instance, public disclosure of a vulnerability before it's patched could leave systems open to exploitation. Ethical hackers must follow responsible disclosure practices and work with the organization to address the vulnerability before revealing it to the public or other hackers.

4. **Dual-Use Tools**
   Many of the tools used by ethical hackers, such as **Metasploit** or **Nmap**, are powerful and can be used for both legitimate security testing and malicious purposes. Ethical hackers must be cautious in their use of these tools, ensuring that they only use them

80

in environments where they have permission and for the purposes of strengthening security.

---

## Conclusion: The Importance of Ethical Hacking in Cybersecurity

Ethical hacking is essential for identifying vulnerabilities, protecting sensitive data, and strengthening the defenses of systems against malicious attacks. Ethical hackers help organizations stay one step ahead of cybercriminals by proactively testing systems for weaknesses and ensuring that security protocols are strong. While ethical hacking presents unique challenges, such as obtaining permission and managing disclosure, it is a critical component of a comprehensive cybersecurity strategy.

As the threat landscape continues to evolve, the need for skilled ethical hackers will only increase. By understanding the ethical boundaries and responsibilities that come with hacking, cybersecurity professionals can help create a safer digital world while maintaining the trust and security of the organizations they protect.

This chapter provides an overview of ethical hacking, its role in cybersecurity, real-world examples, and the ethical challenges that ethical hackers face.

# CHAPTER 7

# TOOLS OF THE TRADE

## Introduction: The Essential Tools for Ethical Hackers and Security Analysts

In cybersecurity, the right tools are essential for identifying vulnerabilities, assessing risks, and protecting systems from cyberattacks. Ethical hackers and security analysts rely on a variety of specialized tools to perform their duties. These tools enable professionals to conduct penetration tests, monitor networks, analyze traffic, and secure sensitive data. Whether you're scanning for vulnerabilities, sniffing network traffic, or testing the resilience of a system, knowing how to use the right tool for the job is a critical skill in the cybersecurity profession.

This chapter will explore some of the most widely used tools in the cybersecurity industry, including **Kali Linux**, **Metasploit**, **Wireshark**, and **Nmap**, as well as explain how these tools are applied in real-world security assessments.

**Essential Tools for Ethical Hackers and Security Analysts**

1. **Kali**                                      **Linux**

   Kali Linux is a **Debian-based Linux distribution** specifically designed for penetration testing and security auditing. It comes pre-installed with a comprehensive suite of security tools, making it a go-to resource for ethical hackers and security professionals.

   **Key Features**:

   - o **Pre-installed Security Tools**: Kali Linux includes over 600 tools for various cybersecurity tasks, such as vulnerability scanning, wireless analysis, password cracking, and more.
   - o **Customizable and Open-Source**: Kali is open-source, which allows users to customize it to their specific needs, adding or removing tools as necessary.
   - o **Live Boot Capability**: Kali can be run from a USB stick, making it portable and easy to use on different systems without installation.

84

**Real-World Use Case**: Ethical hackers use Kali Linux to conduct **penetration tests** on networks and systems. The pre-installed tools, such as **Aircrack-ng** for Wi-Fi security testing and **Burp Suite** for web application vulnerability scanning, allow hackers to simulate attacks and identify weaknesses.

**Example**: In 2019, a security consultant used Kali Linux to test the resilience of a client's internal network by running a vulnerability scan using **Nikto** (a web server scanner). The scan identified several misconfigurations in the server that were promptly patched.

2. **Metasploit**

   **Metasploit** is a powerful framework used for developing and executing exploit code against remote target machines. It is widely used in penetration testing and for conducting controlled security assessments.

   **Key Features**:

- o **Exploit Development**: Metasploit allows ethical hackers to create and test exploits, which are pieces of code designed to exploit vulnerabilities in systems.
- o **Payloads**: Metasploit includes pre-built payloads that can be delivered to target machines to provide control, like **reverse shells** or **meterpreter** sessions.
- o **Post-Exploitation**: After compromising a system, Metasploit can help maintain access and gather intelligence about the compromised system.

**Real-World Use Case**: Penetration testers often use Metasploit to simulate attacks on an organization's infrastructure to uncover potential security weaknesses. Metasploit can automate the process of delivering exploits and gaining access to vulnerable systems.

**Example**: In a security assessment for a client's internal network, a penetration tester used Metasploit's **exploit modules** to exploit an outdated **Windows SMB vulnerability**, gaining access to sensitive files and proving the need for a patch management system.

3. **Wireshark**

**Wireshark** is a widely-used network protocol analyzer that allows security professionals to capture and inspect data packets traveling across a network. It is a key tool for network monitoring, troubleshooting, and security analysis.

**Key Features**:

- o **Packet Capture**: Wireshark captures network traffic in real-time, allowing users to inspect individual packets for anomalies, malware, and potential vulnerabilities.
- o **Deep Packet Inspection**: Wireshark provides detailed information about the network protocols being used, such as **TCP, UDP, HTTP**, and more.
- o **Filtering Capabilities**: Users can filter captured packets based on criteria like IP addresses, ports, and protocols to focus on specific traffic.

87

**Real-World Use Case**: Wireshark is often used to analyze network traffic and identify suspicious activity. Security analysts use Wireshark to detect and analyze signs of cyberattacks, such as **man-in-the-middle (MitM) attacks**, **denial-of-service (DoS) attacks**, and **data exfiltration**.

**Example**: A network analyst at a financial institution used Wireshark to monitor traffic during a **phishing attack**. By inspecting packets, they identified that the attacker was attempting to steal **login credentials** by capturing **HTTP traffic** (unencrypted). This prompted the organization to switch to **HTTPS** encryption.

4. **Nmap (Network Mapper)**
**Nmap** is a powerful open-source tool used for network discovery and vulnerability scanning. It is primarily used to scan networks, identify devices, and detect open ports that may be vulnerable to attacks.

**Key Features**:

- o **Port Scanning**: Nmap allows security professionals to identify open ports on a target system, which can help identify potential entry points for cyberattacks.
- o **OS Detection**: Nmap can detect the **operating systems** running on remote devices, providing crucial information during a penetration test.
- o **Service Version Detection**: It can also detect the versions of services running on open ports, allowing hackers to identify whether those services have known vulnerabilities.

**Real-World     Use     Case**: Nmap is frequently used by ethical hackers to gather reconnaissance on a target network before performing deeper penetration testing. By scanning the network and identifying open ports, hackers can determine potential attack vectors.

**Example**: During a security audit for a client's corporate network, a penetration tester used Nmap to identify open ports and found that an **SSH** service was exposed to the internet without proper access controls. This finding allowed the tester to further investigate potential vulnerabilities in the SSH service.

---

**How These Tools Are Used in Real-World Security Assessments**

The tools discussed above are regularly employed in real-world security assessments to evaluate the security posture of an organization. Here's how these tools come together in a typical penetration testing or security audit scenario:

1. **Reconnaissance and Scanning**
   The first phase of a penetration test involves gathering information about the target system or network. Tools like **Nmap** are used to perform a **network scan**, identifying live hosts, open ports, and services running on the target system. **Wireshark** may be used to monitor network traffic and look for any suspicious activity that might give further insights into the target environment.

2. **Vulnerability Identification and Exploitation**
   After gathering information, ethical hackers use tools like **Metasploit** to test for vulnerabilities within the

90

system. If vulnerabilities are identified, the penetration tester may use **Metasploit**'s exploit modules to attempt to gain access to the system. In this stage, ethical hackers simulate real-world attacks to demonstrate the level of risk the organization faces.

3. **Post-Exploitation and Reporting**
   Once access is gained, ethical hackers use tools like **Metasploit** and **Wireshark** to maintain access, gather data, and assess the depth of the breach. Post-exploitation tools help ethical hackers determine the potential impact of an attack. Ethical hackers then prepare reports detailing the vulnerabilities found, the methods used to exploit them, and recommendations for securing the system.

4. **Remediation and Retesting**
   After the penetration test is complete, the security team works on fixing the identified vulnerabilities. Once remediation is done, ethical hackers retest the system to ensure the vulnerabilities are fully patched and that no new security gaps have been introduced.

**Conclusion**

The tools of the trade are crucial for ethical hackers and security analysts as they work to identify and mitigate cyber risks. **Kali Linux**, **Metasploit**, **Wireshark**, and **Nmap** are just a few examples of the powerful tools that enable cybersecurity professionals to perform penetration tests, monitor network traffic, and secure systems. Mastering these tools is key to becoming proficient in ethical hacking and contributing to a more secure digital landscape.

In the next chapters, we will continue to explore more advanced tools and techniques used in specific cybersecurity roles, helping you further develop your skills and expertise in the field.

---

This chapter covers essential cybersecurity tools and their real-world applications.

# CHAPTER 8

# NETWORKING AND OPERATING SYSTEMS BASICS

## Introduction: The Foundation of Cybersecurity

A solid understanding of networking and operating systems (OS) is fundamental for anyone pursuing a career in cybersecurity. Network protocols, operating systems, and how they interact play a central role in safeguarding digital infrastructure and protecting sensitive data. If you're considering a career in cybersecurity, it's essential to grasp the basic concepts of networking and operating systems because many cyberattacks exploit flaws in these areas.

In this chapter, we'll dive into networking fundamentals and examine the operating systems commonly used in cybersecurity. We'll also explore real-life examples of network vulnerabilities and OS misconfigurations to highlight the importance of understanding these concepts for successful security practices.

**A Deep Dive Into Networking Fundamentals and Why They Matter for Cybersecurity**

1. **What is Networking?**
   Networking refers to the practice of connecting computers, devices, and systems to share resources and communicate with each other. It involves various technologies, protocols, and devices that enable data transfer between systems. In cybersecurity, understanding how networks function is essential for identifying and preventing threats.

   **Key Components of Networking**:

   o **IP Addressing**: Each device on a network is assigned a unique **IP address**. Understanding how to configure and secure IP addresses is critical to ensuring that only authorized devices can connect to a network.

   o **Subnetting**: Subnetting divides large networks into smaller, manageable subnetworks (subnets), improving security by isolating devices and controlling traffic flow.

- o **Routing**: Routers are devices that direct data packets between devices on different networks. Understanding how routers function helps ethical hackers understand how to gain unauthorized access or block malicious traffic.

- o **Switches**: Switches operate within a network to connect devices. While switches work within a local network, they play an important role in network segmentation and monitoring traffic.

2. **Key Network Protocols to Understand**
Networking protocols define the rules for data communication. Understanding how these protocols work is essential for recognizing vulnerabilities and securing networks.

**Important Protocols**:

- o **TCP/IP (Transmission Control Protocol/Internet Protocol)**: The fundamental protocol for internet and network communication. Understanding the layers of **TCP/IP** (application, transport, internet, and link) allows you to troubleshoot network issues and secure communication channels.

- o **DNS (Domain Name System)**: DNS translates domain names (like **example.com**) into IP addresses. Exploiting vulnerabilities in DNS can enable attackers to redirect traffic to malicious sites (**DNS spoofing** or **cache poisoning**).

- o **HTTP/HTTPS (Hypertext Transfer Protocol)**: HTTP is used to transfer web pages, and HTTPS secures the connection with encryption. Attacks like **man-in-the-middle (MitM)** can occur when sensitive data is transmitted over unsecured HTTP.

- o **FTP (File Transfer Protocol)**: FTP is used to transfer files across a network. FTP lacks encryption, making it a common target for attackers who can intercept or alter file transfers.

**Real-World                                    Example**: In **2016**, a massive **DDoS (Distributed Denial-of-Service)** attack targeted **Dyn**, a DNS provider, using a botnet made up of **IoT devices**. This attack exploited weak security in networked devices and targeted DNS servers, causing disruptions for major websites like **Twitter**, **Reddit**, and **Spotify**. Understanding DNS security and how DDoS attacks operate could have mitigated the impact of this attack.

3. **Network Security Tools**
Security professionals use various tools to monitor and protect network infrastructure. **Firewalls, Intrusion Detection Systems (IDS)**, and **Intrusion Prevention Systems (IPS)** are common tools for defending against unauthorized access and attacks. Understanding how these tools work and how to configure them effectively is vital for cybersecurity professionals.

**A Look at Operating Systems Used in Cybersecurity: Linux and Windows**

1. **Linux**
Linux is an open-source operating system widely used by cybersecurity professionals. It's known for its stability, flexibility, and security features. Most

ethical hackers prefer Linux for conducting penetration tests and vulnerability assessments because it allows deep customization and provides access to powerful tools like **Kali Linux**, **Metasploit**, and **Nmap**.

**Why Linux is Important for Cybersecurity**:

o **Customizability**: Linux allows users to tailor the operating system to their specific needs, providing full control over security settings and configurations.

o **Command Line Interface (CLI)**: The command line in Linux is a powerful tool for network and system administration, essential for ethical hackers who need to perform tasks like network scanning, vulnerability testing, and system monitoring.

o **Security Features**: Linux offers advanced security features, such as **AppArmor** and **SELinux**, that can help protect systems from unauthorized access.

**Real-World** **Example**:
**Penetration testers** often use Linux-based

98

distributions like **Kali Linux** or **Parrot Security OS** to perform **security audits** on organizations' systems. These distributions come with pre-installed security tools that help ethical hackers identify vulnerabilities in applications, networks, and databases.

2. **Windows**

Windows is one of the most widely used operating systems in enterprise environments. It's important for cybersecurity professionals to understand Windows security, as many organizations rely on it for their business infrastructure. Windows is often targeted by attackers because of its widespread use and the complexity of its system.

**Why Windows is Important for Cybersecurity**:

- o **Widely Used**: Many organizations and individuals use Windows, making it a common target for cyberattacks. Cybersecurity professionals must be familiar with Windows security vulnerabilities to protect systems.

99

- o **Windows Defender**: Windows includes built-in security features like **Windows Defender** (antivirus and malware protection) and **BitLocker** (full-disk encryption). Understanding how to configure these tools is important for securing systems.
- o **Active Directory**: Windows is commonly used in environments with **Active Directory**, which controls user access and permissions across an organization's network. Misconfigurations in Active Directory can lead to serious security breaches.

**Real-World                    Example**:
In **2017**, the **WannaCry ransomware** attack primarily affected Windows systems. The attack exploited a vulnerability in Windows' **SMB (Server Message Block)** protocol, allowing ransomware to spread across vulnerable networks. Microsoft had released a patch months before the attack, but many systems had not been updated. This highlighted the importance of patch management in Windows environments.

3. **Mac** **OS**

While less common in enterprise environments, **Mac OS** (Apple's operating system) is widely used in creative industries and by individual consumers. Cybersecurity professionals should also understand the security features of Mac OS, especially as the operating system becomes more targeted by attackers due to its growing popularity.

---

**Real-Life Examples of Network Vulnerabilities and Operating System Misconfigurations**

1. **Heartbleed** **Vulnerability** **(2014)**

The **Heartbleed vulnerability** was a flaw in **OpenSSL**, an encryption protocol widely used to secure internet communications. Heartbleed allowed attackers to exploit a weakness in the implementation of **TLS/SSL encryption**, potentially exposing sensitive data like passwords, private keys, and credit card information. This vulnerability affected both Linux and Windows servers, demonstrating how misconfigurations in security protocols can put systems at risk.

101

2. **Windows SMB Vulnerability (WannaCry, 2017)**

   The WannaCry ransomware attack exploited a vulnerability in the **SMBv1** protocol used by Windows systems. The vulnerability, identified as **CVE-2017-0144**, allowed attackers to spread ransomware rapidly across networks. While Microsoft had issued a patch months earlier, many organizations had not updated their systems, leading to widespread damage. This highlights the importance of patching systems promptly to prevent attacks.

3. **Misconfigured                              Firewalls**

   Firewalls are essential for protecting networks, but misconfigurations can open the door to attacks. A common vulnerability is the **exposure of unnecessary ports** to the internet, which can provide attackers with an entry point into the network. For instance, an open **SSH port** or **FTP service** could allow attackers to gain unauthorized access to systems. Regularly auditing firewall configurations and closing unnecessary ports is crucial for improving security.

## Conclusion: The Importance of Networking and Operating Systems Knowledge in Cybersecurity

A thorough understanding of networking fundamentals and operating systems is essential for any cybersecurity professional. Networks are the backbone of all communication, and understanding how data flows, which protocols are used, and how to secure network devices is crucial in preventing cyberattacks. Similarly, operating systems like Linux and Windows are the platforms on which most cyberattacks take place, so knowing how to secure and defend these systems is key to effective cybersecurity.

By understanding how vulnerabilities manifest in both networks and operating systems, cybersecurity professionals are better equipped to identify weaknesses, mitigate risks, and respond to potential threats. The next chapter will delve deeper into specific security tools and techniques used to protect these critical systems.

---

This chapter covers the basics of networking and operating systems, their role in cybersecurity, and real-world examples of vulnerabilities and misconfigurations.

# CHAPTER 9

# UNDERSTANDING FIREWALLS, VPNS, AND PROXIES

## Introduction: The Essential Role of Firewalls, VPNs, and Proxies in Cybersecurity

In the digital world, where threats lurk at every corner, protecting data and securing communications are paramount for businesses and individuals alike. Three critical technologies that play an essential role in safeguarding networks and information are **firewalls**, **VPNs (Virtual Private Networks)**, and **proxies**. These tools work in different ways to control traffic, block malicious access, and ensure privacy and security.

In this chapter, we'll explore how firewalls, VPNs, and proxies function to protect networks, discuss real-world use cases where they are effectively employed, and examine the ethical considerations surrounding their use in cybersecurity testing.

## How Firewalls, VPNs, and Proxies Work to Protect Networks

1. **Firewalls: The First Line of Defense**
   A **firewall** is a network security system that monitors and controls incoming and outgoing traffic based on predetermined security rules. Firewalls are the first line of defense against unauthorized access, cyberattacks, and malicious traffic.

   **Key Functions**:

   - **Traffic Filtering**: Firewalls analyze traffic based on criteria like IP addresses, port numbers, and protocols. Traffic that does not meet predefined security rules is blocked.
   - **Packet Inspection**: Firewalls perform **packet filtering**, inspecting data packets at various layers of the OSI model (typically Layer 3 for network firewalls, and Layer 7 for application firewalls).
   - **Stateful Inspection**: Some advanced firewalls are capable of stateful inspection, meaning they track the state of active connections and make decisions based on the

context of those connections (e.g., allowing responses to an outgoing request but blocking unsolicited traffic).

**Types of Firewalls**:

- o **Network Firewalls**: Placed between internal networks and the internet, network firewalls monitor traffic that enters or leaves a network.

- o **Application Firewalls**: These firewalls are used to filter traffic specific to applications (such as web traffic) and protect against threats like SQL injections or cross-site scripting (XSS).

- o **Next-Generation Firewalls (NGFWs)**: NGFWs combine traditional firewall features with additional security features such as intrusion prevention systems (IPS), antivirus filtering, and deep packet inspection (DPI).

**Real-World                    Example**: A **corporate network** uses a **next-generation firewall (NGFW)** to block unauthorized external traffic and monitor internal communications. The firewall is configured to allow traffic only from trusted IP addresses, while blocking access to known malicious IPs and websites. Additionally, the NGFW inspects application traffic to prevent malware from entering the network.

2. **VPNs: Secure Connections Over Untrusted Networks**

A **Virtual Private Network (VPN)** creates a secure, encrypted connection between two endpoints over an untrusted network, such as the internet. VPNs are commonly used to protect sensitive data during transmission, particularly when accessing public or unsecured networks (e.g., public Wi-Fi).

**Key Functions**:

- o **Encryption**: VPNs encrypt the data transmitted between devices, ensuring that even if the data is intercepted, it remains unreadable.

- o **Remote Access**: VPNs allow users to securely connect to a private network (e.g., a company's internal network) from remote locations, maintaining confidentiality and security.

○ **Bypassing Geographic Restrictions**: VPNs can mask a user's IP address and make it appear as though they are accessing the internet from a different location, bypassing geo-restrictions or censorship.

**Real-World** **Example**: A **remote employee** uses a VPN to securely access their company's internal resources (e.g., email, databases) while working from a public coffee shop. The VPN ensures that any data sent over the public Wi-Fi is encrypted, preventing attackers from intercepting sensitive information such as login credentials or proprietary data.

3. **Proxies: Intermediaries for Network Traffic** A **proxy server** acts as an intermediary between a client and the destination server. It forwards requests from the client to the destination server and then returns the response to the client. Proxies can be used to filter traffic, increase privacy, or improve network performance.

**Key Functions**:

- o **Traffic Filtering**: Proxies can filter out unwanted traffic or block access to certain websites by intercepting requests and only allowing specific traffic to pass through.

- o **Privacy and Anonymity**: By masking the client's IP address, proxies can enhance user privacy and anonymity, making it difficult for external systems to trace requests back to the original user.

- o **Caching**: Proxy servers can cache content to improve performance. For example, frequently accessed web pages can be stored locally on the proxy, reducing load times for users.

**Types of Proxies**:

- o **Forward Proxies**: These proxies are placed between the client and the server, forwarding requests from clients to servers.

- o **Reverse Proxies**: These proxies are placed between the server and the client, often used for load balancing and caching.

o **Transparent Proxies**: These proxies intercept traffic without requiring any configuration changes on the client side, typically used for network monitoring or content filtering.

**Real-World** **Example**: A company uses a **reverse proxy** to distribute web traffic across multiple web servers, improving load balancing and increasing the performance and availability of their website. The proxy also hides the identity of the internal web servers, providing an additional layer of security against direct attacks.

---

**Real-World Use Cases: Using Firewalls to Prevent Unauthorized Access**

1. **Preventing DDoS Attacks with Firewalls**
   A **Denial of Service (DoS)** or **Distributed Denial of Service (DDoS)** attack involves overwhelming a target system with traffic, rendering it unavailable to legitimate users. Firewalls can be used to mitigate

these attacks by filtering out malicious traffic and ensuring that only legitimate requests are processed.

**Example**:

An e-commerce company facing a DDoS attack uses a firewall with **rate limiting** capabilities to control the amount of traffic allowed from a single IP address. By blocking or throttling suspicious requests, the firewall helps ensure that the website remains accessible to genuine customers.

2. **Securing Internal Networks with Firewalls**
   Firewalls are also essential for securing internal networks by preventing unauthorized users from accessing sensitive data or systems. By implementing **network segmentation** with firewalls, organizations can restrict access to different network segments based on roles, responsibilities, and trust levels.

**Example**:

A financial institution deploys firewalls to segment its **customer data network** from its **transaction network**. Only authorized personnel can access the transaction network, ensuring that sensitive financial

111

data remains protected from potential breaches or internal threats.

---

**Ethical Considerations When Using VPNs and Proxies in Cybersecurity Testing**

While VPNs and proxies are vital tools for protecting privacy and securing networks, their use in cybersecurity testing presents unique ethical considerations.

1. **VPNs in Cybersecurity Testing**
   When using VPNs in ethical hacking or penetration testing, ethical hackers must ensure they have **explicit authorization** from the organization to conduct the tests. VPNs can be used to simulate an attacker's access from a remote location, but they can also be misused if used to bypass network security measures without proper consent.

   **Ethical Consideration**:
   Using a VPN without authorization to bypass network security could be considered **unauthorized access** and could have legal consequences. Ethical hackers must always operate within the bounds of the

law and obtain written permission before performing any penetration tests or accessing systems remotely via VPN.

2. **Proxies in Penetration Testing**
   Proxies are often used in **web application penetration testing** to intercept and modify HTTP/HTTPS traffic between the client and the server. While proxies like **Burp Suite** are essential for identifying vulnerabilities in web applications, using proxies in ways that bypass security policies or data privacy laws can be ethically problematic.

   **Ethical                                    Consideration**:
   When using proxies to intercept traffic, ethical hackers should ensure they are not capturing or manipulating sensitive data without proper consent. Ethical hackers must adhere to responsible disclosure practices, report vulnerabilities in a way that minimizes risk, and avoid exposing personally identifiable information (PII) or confidential business data.

**Conclusion: Firewalls, VPNs, and Proxies in Cybersecurity**

Firewalls, VPNs, and proxies are integral components of a robust cybersecurity strategy. They play vital roles in **network protection**, **privacy**, and **secure communications**. Whether preventing unauthorized access with firewalls, securing remote connections with VPNs, or enhancing privacy with proxies, these tools are essential for safeguarding digital assets.

As we move forward, it's important to balance the powerful capabilities of these tools with the ethical responsibilities associated with their use in cybersecurity testing. Understanding the ethical implications ensures that cybersecurity professionals maintain trust and integrity while conducting assessments, protecting both systems and sensitive data.

---

This chapter provides a comprehensive overview of firewalls, VPNs, and proxies, along with real-world examples of how they are used in cybersecurity and the ethical considerations that come with their application.

# CHAPTER 10

# CRYPTOGRAPHY: THE SCIENCE OF SECURE COMMUNICATION

## Introduction: The Importance of Cryptography in Cybersecurity

Cryptography is the practice of securing communication and information by transforming it into an unreadable format, ensuring that only authorized parties can access or understand it. In the world of cybersecurity, cryptography plays an essential role in safeguarding sensitive data, verifying the authenticity of information, and maintaining privacy.

In this chapter, we'll explore the basics of cryptography, including **encryption**, **decryption**, and **hashing**, and examine how these techniques are applied in real-world scenarios to protect data. Understanding cryptography is fundamental for anyone working in cybersecurity, as it helps prevent data breaches, identity theft, and cyberattacks.

**The Basics of Cryptography: Encryption, Decryption, and Hashing**

1. **Encryption**

   **Encryption** is the process of converting plaintext (readable data) into ciphertext (unreadable data) using a cryptographic algorithm and a key. The purpose of encryption is to protect data from unauthorized access by ensuring that even if intercepted, the data remains unreadable.

   o **Symmetric Encryption**: In symmetric encryption, the same key is used for both encryption and decryption. This method is faster but requires secure key management. If the key is compromised, the entire system is at risk.

     ▪ **Example**: **AES (Advanced Encryption Standard)** is a widely used symmetric encryption algorithm that is commonly used to encrypt sensitive data like files and communications.

   o **Asymmetric Encryption**: Asymmetric encryption uses a pair of keys—one for encryption (**public key**) and one for decryption (**private key**). This method is slower but more secure because the private key never needs to be shared.

- **Example**: **RSA** and **Elliptic Curve Cryptography (ECC)** are examples of asymmetric encryption algorithms used in applications like secure email and digital signatures.

**Real-World** **Example**:
When you visit a website using **HTTPS**, the communication between your browser and the server is encrypted using **asymmetric encryption**. The server provides a public key that is used to encrypt data sent to it, while the private key ensures that only the server can decrypt the data.

2. **Decryption**

**Decryption** is the reverse process of encryption. It converts the encrypted data (ciphertext) back into its original, readable form (plaintext). Decryption can only occur if the correct key or algorithm is used. In symmetric encryption, the same key is used for both encryption and decryption. In asymmetric encryption, the private key is used to decrypt data

117

that was encrypted with the corresponding public key.

- o **Example**: If you send a file encrypted with AES to someone, they can decrypt the file using the same AES key. In contrast, if you encrypt a message with a public key (asymmetric encryption), only the recipient with the corresponding private key can decrypt it.

3. **Hashing**

   **Hashing** is a one-way process that transforms data into a fixed-length string of characters, called a hash. Unlike encryption, hashing is **irreversible**, meaning you cannot recover the original data from the hash. Hashing is typically used for verifying data integrity and storing passwords securely.

   - o **Cryptographic Hash Functions**: A hash function takes an input (or "message") and returns a fixed-size string, typically represented as a hexadecimal number. Even small changes in the input will produce a completely different hash.

     - ▪ **Example: SHA-256 (Secure Hash Algorithm 256-bit)** is a commonly

118

used cryptographic hash function that generates a 256-bit hash value. It is widely used in blockchain technology to ensure the integrity of data.

**Real-World** **Example**:

When you enter your password on a website, the password is hashed and stored in the website's database. When you log in again, the system hashes the entered password and compares it to the stored hash to verify the correct password without ever storing the plain text version of your password.

## Real-World Examples of Cryptography in Action

1. **HTTPS:** **Securing** **Web** **Traffic**

   One of the most common uses of cryptography is in **HTTPS** (HyperText Transfer Protocol Secure), which is the secure version of HTTP used to transfer data between a web browser and a website. HTTPS uses a combination of **asymmetric encryption** (for key exchange) and **symmetric encryption** (for actual data transfer) to ensure that data sent over the web is encrypted and secure from interception.

**How It Works**:

- When a user accesses a website using HTTPS, the web server sends its **SSL/TLS certificate** (which includes a public key) to the browser.
- The browser uses this public key to encrypt a random session key, which is then sent back to the server. Only the server's private key can decrypt this session key.
- Once the session key is established, it is used to encrypt the entire communication between the browser and the server, ensuring privacy and data integrity.

**Real-World**          **Example**:
When you shop online, you see the **"HTTPS"** at the start of the URL, indicating that the communication between your browser and the online store is encrypted. This encryption prevents attackers from intercepting sensitive information, such as credit

card details and personal data, during the transaction process.

2. **End-to-End Encryption in Messaging Apps**
Many modern messaging apps, such as **WhatsApp**, **Signal**, and **Telegram**, use **end-to-end encryption** (E2EE) to protect the privacy of users' messages. In E2EE, only the sender and the recipient have the keys needed to decrypt the messages. Even the service provider (e.g., WhatsApp) cannot decrypt the messages.

**How It Works**:

- ○ When you send a message, it is encrypted with the recipient's **public key**.
- ○ The recipient can only decrypt the message with their **private key**.
- ○ This process ensures that even if a hacker intercepts the message during transmission, they cannot read its contents.

**Real-World**                                    **Example**:
A journalist uses an encrypted messaging app to communicate securely with a source. The messages

are encrypted end-to-end, ensuring that even if the messages are intercepted, only the journalist and the source can read them.

3. **Digital Signatures: Verifying Authenticity**
Digital signatures are used to verify the authenticity of digital documents and transactions. They rely on **asymmetric encryption** and provide a way for individuals or organizations to prove their identity without sharing their private keys.

**How It Works**:

o A sender creates a hash of the message or document and encrypts it with their **private key**. This creates the **digital signature**.

o The recipient can decrypt the digital signature using the sender's **public key**. If the hash matches the hash of the message, the message is authentic and hasn't been tampered with.

**Real-World** **Example**:
A software developer uses a digital signature to sign a software package before distributing it. When users

download the software, they can verify the signature to ensure that the software hasn't been tampered with and is genuinely from the developer.

## How Encryption Is Used to Protect Sensitive Data

Encryption is one of the most effective ways to protect sensitive data, whether it's being stored on a device or transmitted over a network. By converting readable data into an unreadable format, encryption ensures that only authorized parties can access or understand the information.

1. **Protecting        Data        at        Rest**
   Encryption is commonly used to protect **data at rest**, which refers to data that is stored on a physical device (e.g., hard drives, cloud storage). For example, **BitLocker** (for Windows) and **FileVault** (for macOS) are encryption tools that protect data stored on laptops, ensuring that even if the device is lost or stolen, the data cannot be accessed without the decryption key.

   **Real-World                    Example**:
   A company encrypts all employee laptops with

BitLocker to protect sensitive corporate data. If a laptop is lost or stolen, the data remains encrypted, and unauthorized users cannot access it without the decryption key.

2. **Protecting Data in Transit**
   **Encryption in transit** is used to secure data as it travels over a network. This type of encryption ensures that any sensitive information, such as login credentials, personal data, or payment details, is protected from interception during transmission.

**Real-World Example**:
A user accesses their online bank account using **HTTPS**. The encryption protects their banking credentials and account details from potential eavesdropping, ensuring that the communication remains private even over public networks.

---

## Conclusion: The Science of Secure Communication

Cryptography is the backbone of modern cybersecurity. By understanding the principles of **encryption**, **decryption**, and **hashing**, professionals can protect data, ensure privacy, and maintain the integrity of digital communications. From securing web traffic with **HTTPS** to safeguarding sensitive files with encryption and verifying authenticity with **digital signatures**, cryptography is a critical tool in the fight against cybercrime.

In the next chapters, we will continue exploring how cryptography integrates with other security technologies and techniques to build resilient systems that protect our most valuable information.

---

This chapter provides a comprehensive introduction to cryptography, explaining the basics of encryption, decryption, and hashing, and how these methods are used in real-world applications to secure data. Let me know if you'd like more details on specific cryptographic concepts or examples!

# *CHAPTER 11*

# *VULNERABILITY ASSESSMENT AND PENETRATION TESTING*

### Introduction: Understanding Vulnerability Assessment and Penetration Testing

In the ever-evolving landscape of cybersecurity, discovering and mitigating vulnerabilities is crucial to protecting organizations from malicious cyberattacks. **Vulnerability assessment** and **penetration testing (pen testing)** are two critical components of any security strategy. These practices involve simulating attacks on a system to identify and address weaknesses before real-world hackers can exploit them.

In this chapter, we'll define vulnerability assessment and penetration testing, explain how to conduct a penetration test step-by-step, and provide real-world examples of successful penetration tests and their outcomes.

**What is Vulnerability Assessment and Penetration Testing (Pen Testing)?**

1. **Vulnerability                    Assessment**

   A **vulnerability assessment** is the process of identifying, quantifying, and prioritizing vulnerabilities in a system or network. It involves scanning a system for known weaknesses—such as outdated software, misconfigured settings, or open ports—and assessing the severity of these issues. Vulnerability assessments are typically automated, with tools scanning networks or applications for potential security flaws.

   **Key Features**:

   - **Systematic Scanning**: Vulnerability scanners like **Nessus**, **OpenVAS**, and **Qualys** are used to identify security flaws.
   - **Prioritization**: Vulnerabilities are prioritized based on their potential impact and exploitability, allowing organizations to address the most critical issues first.
   - **Risk Analysis**: Vulnerability assessments help organizations understand the level of

risk they face from each vulnerability, enabling them to make informed decisions about remediation.

**Real-World                        Example**:
An e-commerce company conducts a vulnerability assessment using **Nessus** to scan its web servers and identify vulnerabilities. The scan detects several **outdated software versions** with known security flaws, prompting the company to update its systems to mitigate the risk of an attack.

2. **Penetration      Testing      (Pen      Testing)**
   **Penetration testing** is a simulated cyberattack conducted by ethical hackers to test the defenses of a system, network, or application. Penetration testers (pen testers) use the same tools and techniques as malicious hackers to exploit vulnerabilities and gain unauthorized access to systems. However, unlike actual hackers, pen testers do so with permission from the organization to identify weaknesses that need to be addressed.

**Key Features**:

- o **Simulated Attack**: Penetration testing goes beyond identifying vulnerabilities—it involves actively exploiting those vulnerabilities to assess the potential damage an attacker could cause.

- o **Manual and Automated Testing**: While vulnerability assessments are largely automated, penetration tests often require manual techniques to exploit vulnerabilities and mimic advanced attacks.

- o **Real-World Scenarios**: Penetration testing aims to simulate realistic attack scenarios, including social engineering, phishing attacks, and exploiting software vulnerabilities.

**Real-World** **Example**:
A financial institution hires an ethical hacker to conduct a penetration test on its internal network. The test simulates an attacker exploiting an **unpatched vulnerability** in the bank's **web application**. The ethical hacker gains access to sensitive customer data, demonstrating the need for a security patch.

## How to Conduct a Penetration Test: A Step-by-Step Guide

Penetration testing involves several phases that help identify vulnerabilities, exploit them, and evaluate the system's overall security. Here's a step-by-step guide to conducting a penetration test:

1. **Step 1: Planning and Scoping**
   - **Objective Setting**: Before starting, the tester and the organization define the scope of the engagement. This includes identifying the systems, networks, and applications to be tested and setting clear objectives (e.g., testing web application security or network infrastructure).
   - **Rules of Engagement**: Ethical hackers must establish boundaries and gain explicit written permission to test systems. This ensures that no systems are tested beyond the agreed-upon scope and prevents legal issues.
   - **Timeframe and Reporting**: The testing period should be clearly defined, along with

expectations for regular updates and a final report.

2. **Step 2: Reconnaissance (Information Gathering)**
   - **Passive Reconnaissance**: In this phase, penetration testers gather publicly available information about the target system or network. This can include **domain names, IP addresses, DNS records**, and **social media profiles**. Tools like **Google Dorking** and **whois** lookups can uncover critical information.
   - **Active Reconnaissance**: Active scanning involves probing the network and systems directly. Tools like **Nmap** and **Nessus** are used to identify live hosts, open ports, services, and potential attack vectors.

3. **Step 3: Scanning and Enumeration**
   - **Port Scanning**: The tester uses port scanning tools like **Nmap** to identify open ports on the target system. Each open port represents a potential access point for an attacker.
   - **Vulnerability Scanning**: Tools like **Nessus** or **Qualys** are used to perform automated scans of the system to identify vulnerabilities.

This phase highlights areas that require further testing.

4. **Step 4: Exploitation**

   o **Exploiting Vulnerabilities**: Once vulnerabilities are identified, the tester attempts to exploit them to gain access to the system. Exploitation can involve techniques such as **SQL injection**, **buffer overflow**, or exploiting weak passwords.

   o **Using Exploitation Frameworks**: Tools like **Metasploit** and **Burp Suite** can automate the exploitation process and provide useful payloads for gaining unauthorized access.

   o **Privilege Escalation**: After gaining access, the tester attempts to escalate their privileges to gain more control over the system. This could involve exploiting misconfigured permissions or taking advantage of weaknesses in the operating system.

5. **Step 5: Post-Exploitation**

   o **Maintaining Access**: Once the tester gains access, they attempt to maintain that access by creating **backdoors** or adding **user**

**accounts** that could be used for future attacks.

- ○ **Data Extraction**: Pen testers may attempt to extract sensitive data, such as passwords, database contents, or customer information, to demonstrate the potential risk of an attack.

6. **Step 6: Reporting and Remediation**

- ○ **Detailed Report**: After completing the test, penetration testers compile a detailed report outlining the findings, including the vulnerabilities discovered, methods used to exploit them, and the potential impact of the attack.

- ○ **Recommendations for Remediation**: The report includes recommendations for fixing the identified vulnerabilities, such as patching software, enhancing authentication measures, or reconfiguring network defenses.

- ○ **Retesting**: After the vulnerabilities are addressed, penetration testers may be asked to retest the system to ensure that the fixes are effective and that no new vulnerabilities were introduced.

**Real-World Examples of Successful Penetration Tests and Their Outcomes**

1. **The eBay Penetration Test (2014)**
   **eBay** conducted a **penetration test** to assess its security posture after receiving warnings from its security team about potential weaknesses. The penetration test revealed that attackers could exploit a **vulnerable web application** and gain access to user accounts. By exploiting **SQL injection** vulnerabilities, ethical hackers were able to retrieve sensitive data, such as user passwords and email addresses.

   **Outcome**:
   eBay implemented stronger input validation and SQL injection prevention mechanisms, including **prepared statements** in database queries, to prevent similar attacks in the future. The test helped eBay improve its web application security and safeguard user data.

2. **The Uber Penetration Test (2016)**
   In 2016, **Uber** conducted a penetration test to evaluate the security of its mobile application and

user accounts. The test uncovered several weaknesses in the way the app handled user authentication and session management. By exploiting these weaknesses, ethical hackers were able to gain unauthorized access to Uber's internal network and retrieve sensitive information, including data on drivers and passengers.

**Outcome**:

Uber responded by implementing stronger **multi-factor authentication (MFA)** for both users and internal systems. Additionally, the company improved its session management processes and added extra layers of encryption to protect sensitive data during transmission.

3. **The Target Data Breach (2013)**
   One of the most well-known examples of a penetration test exposing critical vulnerabilities is the **Target data breach** of 2013. Although the breach was not a result of a penetration test, the company's vulnerability was identified during routine security assessments and scans. Attackers exploited weak security in Target's **point-of-sale**

**(POS)** systems to steal credit card information from millions of customers.

**Outcome**:

Following the breach, Target revamped its cybersecurity program, focusing on improving its **network segmentation** and patch management processes. The company also implemented stronger encryption methods for **credit card transactions** and **tokenization** to protect sensitive data.

## Conclusion: The Importance of Vulnerability Assessment and Penetration Testing

Vulnerability assessment and penetration testing are critical components of any cybersecurity strategy. Vulnerability assessments provide a broad view of potential risks in an organization's systems, while penetration testing offers a more hands-on, real-world approach to assessing the effectiveness of security defenses. Together, these methods help organizations identify weaknesses, mitigate risks, and ensure that their systems are prepared to withstand cyberattacks.

By following the step-by-step guide to conducting a penetration test and learning from real-world examples, cybersecurity professionals can develop the skills necessary to protect organizations from malicious threats and safeguard valuable data.

---

This chapter introduces vulnerability assessment and penetration testing, providing a clear, actionable guide for performing penetration tests and showcasing real-world examples of successful assessments.

# CHAPTER 12

# CYBERSECURITY FRAMEWORKS AND STANDARDS

## Introduction: The Importance of Cybersecurity Frameworks and Standards

In the complex world of cybersecurity, frameworks and standards provide organizations with structured approaches to securing their information systems and protecting sensitive data. These frameworks are essential for managing risk, ensuring compliance with regulations, and implementing effective security practices. By adhering to recognized frameworks and standards, organizations can create consistent and repeatable processes to mitigate risks and defend against cyberattacks.

In this chapter, we will explore key cybersecurity frameworks—**NIST, ISO 27001**, and **CIS Controls**—and how they are used by organizations to enhance their security posture. We will also look at real-life examples of organizations implementing these frameworks and the tangible outcomes they have experienced.

**Understanding Cybersecurity Frameworks: NIST, ISO 27001, and CIS Controls**

1. **NIST (National Institute of Standards and Technology) Cybersecurity Framework**

   The **NIST Cybersecurity Framework** is a set of guidelines designed to help organizations improve their ability to detect, respond to, and recover from cyber incidents. Initially developed to address the needs of critical infrastructure, it has since been adopted by organizations of all sizes and industries.

   **Key Components of the NIST Framework:**

   - **Identify**: Develop an understanding of the organization's cybersecurity risks, including assets, resources, and vulnerabilities.
   - **Protect**: Implement safeguards to limit or contain the impact of potential cybersecurity incidents, such as access control and data encryption.
   - **Detect**: Monitor systems to detect cybersecurity events as soon as they occur.

139

- o **Respond**: Take action to contain and mitigate the impact of an incident once it has been detected.
- o **Recover**: Develop strategies to restore any capabilities or services that were disrupted by the cyber incident.

**Real-World** **Example**: **A healthcare organization** adopts the NIST Cybersecurity Framework to better secure patient data. By identifying critical assets and vulnerabilities in its systems, implementing access controls, and establishing robust monitoring and response plans, the organization strengthens its defenses against potential cyberattacks, such as ransomware, and improves its incident response time.

2. **ISO 27001: Information Security Management System (ISMS)** **ISO 27001** is an internationally recognized standard for establishing, implementing, operating, monitoring, reviewing, and improving an **Information Security Management System (ISMS)**. It provides a systematic approach to

managing sensitive company information, ensuring its confidentiality, integrity, and availability.

**Key Features of ISO 27001**:

- o **Risk Management**: ISO 27001 requires organizations to assess and manage risks to the confidentiality, integrity, and availability of information.
- o **Control Objectives**: The standard includes a set of control objectives and security controls that organizations should implement to mitigate risks.
- o **Continuous Improvement**: ISO 27001 encourages organizations to continuously monitor and improve their security practices.

**Real-World                      Example**:
**A global financial services firm** implements the ISO 27001 standard to enhance its data protection practices. After obtaining certification, the company improves its internal security processes, such as risk assessments, employee training, and incident handling procedures, ensuring compliance with

regulatory requirements and securing customer financial data.

3. **CIS Controls (Center for Internet Security Controls)**

The **CIS Controls** are a set of prioritized actions organizations can take to defend their information systems and data from cyber threats. The **CIS Top 20 Controls** are a widely adopted set of best practices designed to provide organizations with practical, actionable guidance on cybersecurity.

**Key Features of CIS Controls**:

- o **Basic Controls**: The first **Critical Security Controls** are focused on basic hygiene practices such as inventory control, continuous vulnerability assessment, and secure configuration management.
- o **Advanced Controls**: As organizations mature in their cybersecurity efforts, they can implement more advanced controls, such as penetration testing, threat intelligence, and security monitoring.

142

o **Practical Guidance**: The CIS Controls are designed to be simple to implement, making them accessible to organizations of all sizes.

**Real-World** **Example**: **A small e-commerce company** applies the CIS Controls to improve its cybersecurity posture. By implementing the foundational controls, such as asset inventory management, continuous vulnerability scanning, and securing remote access, the company significantly reduces its risk of a successful attack, even with limited resources.

## How Organizations Use These Frameworks to Secure Their Environments

Organizations across various industries rely on these cybersecurity frameworks to build robust security programs and ensure the confidentiality, integrity, and availability of their data. Here's how companies typically use each framework:

1. **NIST Cybersecurity Framework**

- o **Risk Management**: NIST helps organizations understand the cybersecurity risks they face by identifying critical assets and assessing vulnerabilities.

- o **Continuous Monitoring**: NIST's **Detect** and **Respond** functions guide organizations in establishing continuous monitoring capabilities to identify threats in real-time.

- o **Incident Response Planning**: NIST assists organizations in developing clear and actionable plans for responding to incidents, including containment strategies and recovery procedures.

2. **ISO 27001**

- o **ISMS Implementation**: ISO 27001 helps organizations establish and operate an ISMS, ensuring they have a systematic approach to managing information security.

- o **Compliance**: Many industries and regions require organizations to comply with certain standards. ISO 27001 provides a globally recognized certification that demonstrates an organization's commitment to cybersecurity and information protection.

- o **Security Audits and Risk Assessments**: ISO 27001 mandates regular security audits and risk assessments to ensure that information security risks are consistently managed and mitigated.

3. **CIS Controls**

   - o **Prioritization**: The **CIS Top 20 Controls** provide organizations with a prioritized list of actions to improve their security posture. This allows organizations, especially small businesses with limited resources, to focus on the most critical areas first.

   - o **Practical Guidance**: The CIS Controls provide straightforward, actionable steps that organizations can implement quickly to improve their cybersecurity hygiene and reduce the likelihood of an attack.

   - o **Automation and Monitoring**: Advanced controls, like security monitoring and automated patch management, help organizations stay ahead of emerging threats and ensure continuous protection.

**Real-Life Examples of Companies Implementing These Standards**

1. **Bank of America and NIST Cybersecurity Framework**

   **Bank of America** adopted the **NIST Cybersecurity Framework** to enhance its security posture and ensure regulatory compliance. By following the NIST guidelines, the bank improved its ability to detect cyber threats and mitigate risks. The bank focused on developing an incident response plan, establishing stronger access control measures, and continuously improving its security practices to protect sensitive financial data.

   **Outcome**:

   As a result, Bank of America was able to significantly reduce the risk of data breaches and enhance its ability to recover from cyber incidents. The bank also met the cybersecurity requirements set forth by regulators, ensuring compliance and improving stakeholder confidence.

2. **Amazon Web Services (AWS) and ISO 27001**

   **Amazon Web Services (AWS)** implemented **ISO**

**27001** to secure its cloud infrastructure and protect customer data. By adhering to ISO 27001, AWS demonstrated its commitment to information security and achieved certification for its global operations. The standard helped AWS establish a comprehensive information security management system (ISMS), covering areas like risk management, vulnerability assessment, and incident response.

**Outcome**:

AWS's implementation of ISO 27001 helped the company gain the trust of its clients, especially those in highly regulated industries like finance and healthcare. The certification allowed AWS to maintain a competitive edge in the cloud services market by ensuring that its infrastructure met rigorous security standards.

3. **Target and CIS Controls**
   After the infamous data breach in 2013, **Target** adopted the **CIS Controls** to strengthen its security practices and prevent future incidents. The company focused on the **Basic Controls**, including network segmentation, vulnerability scanning, and strengthening access management. Target also

implemented continuous monitoring to detect anomalies in real-time.

**Outcome**:

By applying the CIS Controls, Target improved its network defenses and significantly reduced the risk of unauthorized access to its systems. The company also regained customer trust by implementing more stringent security measures and demonstrating a commitment to protecting sensitive data.

## Conclusion: The Role of Cybersecurity Frameworks and Standards

Cybersecurity frameworks and standards, such as **NIST**, **ISO 27001**, and **CIS Controls**, provide organizations with structured approaches to manage cybersecurity risks, comply with regulations, and implement best practices. By using these frameworks, organizations can build robust security programs, detect vulnerabilities, and respond effectively to incidents.

As cyber threats continue to evolve, it is essential for organizations to continually review and update their security strategies. By leveraging these frameworks, businesses can stay ahead of emerging threats, protect sensitive data, and maintain the trust of their customers and stakeholders.

---

This chapter covers the essential cybersecurity frameworks and standards, providing practical insights into how organizations implement these frameworks to secure their environments.

# CHAPTER 13

# THE WORLD OF MALWARE

## Introduction: Understanding Malware and Its Impact

Malware (malicious software) is designed to infiltrate, damage, or disrupt computer systems and networks. As the digital world evolves, so does the sophistication of malware, making it one of the most dangerous threats to both individuals and organizations. Understanding the types of malware, their methods of attack, and how ethical hackers defend against them is crucial for any cybersecurity professional.

In this chapter, we'll explore the various types of malware, real-world examples of significant malware attacks, and how ethical hackers play a critical role in defending against these threats.

## The Types of Malware: Viruses, Worms, Trojans, Ransomware, and More

Malware comes in many forms, each with distinct behaviors and methods of infecting systems. Here are some of the most common types:

1. **Viruses**

   A **virus** is a type of malware that attaches itself to a legitimate program or file. Once the infected file is executed, the virus is activated and can spread to other files, programs, or systems. Viruses can be designed to corrupt data, steal information, or cause systems to crash.

   o **How it Works**: A virus typically spreads by attaching itself to executable files or documents that are shared between users. When the infected file is opened, the virus executes and spreads further.

   o **Real-World Example**: The **ILOVEYOU virus** (2000) spread rapidly through email by disguising itself as a love letter. It caused significant damage by overwriting files and sending itself to everyone in the victim's address book.

2. **Worms**

   **Worms** are similar to viruses, but they differ in that they don't require a host file to propagate. Worms can spread autonomously across networks, exploiting vulnerabilities in software or operating systems to infect other machines without any user interaction.

- **How it Works**: Worms exploit security flaws in systems to spread through email attachments, network shares, or vulnerabilities in applications. They can quickly spread across networks, causing disruptions and overloads.

- **Real-World Example**: The **Conficker worm** (2008) infected millions of computers worldwide, exploiting vulnerabilities in the Windows operating system. It spread through network shares and USB drives, creating a massive botnet used for malicious purposes.

3. **Trojans**

   **Trojans**, also known as **Trojan horses**, are malware that masquerades as legitimate software to trick users into downloading or installing it. Once installed, a Trojan can steal sensitive information, open backdoors for other malware, or grant unauthorized access to systems.

- o **How it Works**: Trojans are often disguised as useful or harmless programs (e.g., software updates, game cracks) and rely on social engineering to persuade users to install them.

- o **Real-World Example**: The **Emotet Trojan** (2014) started as a banking Trojan but evolved into a **botnet** used for distributing other types of malware, including ransomware and information stealers, by exploiting email phishing techniques.

4. **Ransomware**

**Ransomware** is a type of malware that encrypts the victim's files and demands a ransom payment to restore access to the files. Ransomware attacks can be devastating for individuals and organizations, as they often result in significant data loss and financial costs.

- o **How it Works**: Ransomware usually spreads through phishing emails or malicious websites. Once installed, it encrypts files on the victim's computer and demands a payment (usually in cryptocurrency) for decryption keys.

- o **Real-World Example**: The **WannaCry ransomware** attack (2017) exploited a Windows vulnerability to infect over 200,000 computers across 150 countries. The attack encrypted critical data and disrupted healthcare services, including the UK's **NHS**, causing millions in damages.

5. **Spyware and Adware**

**Spyware** and **adware** are types of malware designed to monitor users' activity and display unwanted advertisements. Spyware often tracks personal information, such as browsing habits, login credentials, and credit card details, while adware serves intrusive ads on the user's device.

- o **How it Works**: Spyware silently monitors and collects data, while adware bombards the user with unwanted ads. Both types can degrade system performance and compromise privacy.
- o **Real-World Example**: The **CoolWebSearch** spyware (early 2000s) hijacked web browsers and redirected users to ad-laden websites, stealing search queries and personal data in the process.

154

6. **Rootkits**

A **rootkit** is a type of malware that allows attackers to gain administrator-level (root) access to a system and hide their activities. Rootkits are often difficult to detect because they are designed to operate undetected by conventional security measures.

- **How it Works**: Rootkits often exploit vulnerabilities in operating systems or applications to gain persistent access and conceal malicious processes or files from the user or security software.

- **Real-World Example**: The **Stuxnet** worm (2010), which targeted Iran's nuclear program, used a sophisticated rootkit to hide its presence and disable critical infrastructure without detection.

---

**Real-World Examples of Major Malware Attacks**

1. **WannaCry Ransomware Attack (2017)**
   **WannaCry** was one of the most widespread ransomware attacks in history, affecting over 200,000 computers across 150 countries. It exploited

155

a vulnerability in the **Windows SMB** protocol, which had been discovered by the **NSA** and later leaked to the public by a hacker group known as **Shadow Brokers**. The attack disrupted critical services, particularly in the **UK's National Health Service (NHS)**, causing massive data loss, delayed surgeries, and a total operational shutdown in some areas.

**Outcome**:

The WannaCry attack highlighted the importance of keeping systems updated and patching vulnerabilities in a timely manner. Microsoft had released a patch months before the attack, but many organizations had failed to implement it.

2.  **NotPetya Ransomware (2017)** **NotPetya** was a sophisticated ransomware attack initially targeting Ukrainian organizations, but it quickly spread worldwide. Unlike traditional ransomware, NotPetya was designed to cause permanent damage rather than just extort ransom payments. It used a combination of the **EternalBlue** vulnerability (exploited by WannaCry) and

**Mimikatz** (a tool for stealing credentials) to propagate and infect systems.

**Outcome**:

The attack caused widespread damage to global corporations, including **Maersk** (a shipping giant) and **Merck** (a pharmaceutical company). The total economic impact was estimated at over **$10 billion**, making NotPetya one of the most costly cyberattacks in history.

3. **The SolarWinds Supply Chain Attack (2020)**
   **SolarWinds** was a supply chain attack in which hackers inserted malicious code into the software updates of the **SolarWinds Orion** network management platform. The attack allowed the hackers to gain unauthorized access to the networks of over 18,000 organizations, including government agencies like the **U.S. Department of Homeland Security** and private companies like **Microsoft**.

**Outcome**:

The SolarWinds hack is considered one of the most sophisticated cyberattacks ever discovered. It demonstrated the potential risks of supply chain

157

vulnerabilities and the need for organizations to rigorously secure third-party software and systems.

---

**How Ethical Hackers Defend Against Malware Attacks**

Ethical hackers play a key role in defending against malware attacks by proactively identifying vulnerabilities, simulating attacks, and helping organizations strengthen their defenses. Here's how ethical hackers contribute to malware defense:

1. **Malware                                        Analysis**
   Ethical hackers reverse-engineer malware to understand how it works and how it spreads. By studying the code of malware, they can develop signatures that help antivirus and security software identify and remove it. This also helps in creating better defenses to prevent future attacks.

2. **Penetration Testing and Vulnerability Scanning**
   Ethical hackers use **penetration testing** to simulate how malware could exploit vulnerabilities in an organization's systems. They identify weak spots in security configurations, network architecture, and employee behavior (e.g., falling for phishing attacks)

and recommend improvements to minimize the risk of malware infections.

3. **Implementing Malware Defense Tools**
Ethical hackers recommend and deploy tools such as **firewalls, antivirus software, intrusion detection systems (IDS),** and **endpoint protection** to help organizations detect and block malware. They also emphasize the importance of **regular software updates** and **patch management** to prevent malware from exploiting known vulnerabilities.

4. **Security Awareness Training**
Many malware infections are caused by human error, such as clicking on malicious links or opening infected email attachments. Ethical hackers often work with organizations to provide **security awareness training** to employees, teaching them how to recognize and avoid malware-laden emails, websites, and files.

---

### Conclusion: The Ever-Evolving World of Malware

Malware continues to be one of the most significant threats to cybersecurity. As cybercriminals become more sophisticated, so too must the tools and strategies used to defend against them. Ethical hackers play a critical role in protecting systems from malware by identifying vulnerabilities, testing defenses, and recommending best practices for prevention.

By understanding the various types of malware and real-world examples of successful attacks, organizations can better prepare for future threats and enhance their overall security posture. As cyber threats evolve, so must our approach to combating them, ensuring that we stay one step ahead of attackers.

---

This chapter provides an overview of malware types, real-world examples of attacks, and how ethical hackers defend against malware threats. Let me know if you'd like more detailed examples or further discussion on any of the topics!

# CHAPTER 14

# SOCIAL ENGINEERING AND PHISHING ATTACKS

## Introduction: Understanding Social Engineering and Phishing

Cyber security isn't just about protecting systems, software, and hardware. It's also about protecting people. **Social engineering** is a method of manipulating individuals into performing actions or divulging confidential information that compromises their security. Unlike traditional cyberattacks that rely on exploiting technical vulnerabilities, social engineering exploits human psychology and trust.

One of the most common forms of social engineering is **phishing**, where attackers impersonate legitimate entities to trick victims into revealing sensitive information, like usernames, passwords, or credit card details. In this chapter, we'll explore how social engineering is used in cyberattacks, dive into real-world phishing examples, and discuss how individuals and organizations can recognize and prevent these attacks.

**What is Social Engineering and How Is It Used in Cyber-attacks?**

**Social engineering** is the art of deceiving or manipulating people into making security mistakes or disclosing confidential information. Unlike malware that relies on exploiting system vulnerabilities, social engineering targets the human element, leveraging factors such as trust, fear, urgency, or curiosity.

**Common Tactics Used in Social Engineering**:

1. **Pretexting**: Attackers create a fabricated scenario (pretext) to obtain information or gain access to systems. For example, an attacker might pose as an IT technician to ask for login credentials or security information.

2. **Baiting**: Attackers offer something enticing, such as free software, to lure victims into performing actions that compromise their security. Baiting can involve the use of infected USB drives or fake downloads that install malware when accessed.

3. **Tailgating**: This is a physical form of social engineering where an attacker gains physical access to a restricted area by following someone who has legitimate access, often using a tactic like pretending to be in a rush or carrying heavy items.

4. **Phishing**: Phishing is one of the most common and widespread forms of social engineering. In phishing, attackers send fraudulent messages, often disguised as legitimate communications, to trick the recipient into disclosing personal information, such as usernames, passwords, or financial details.

5. **Vishing (Voice Phishing)**: Similar to phishing, vishing occurs over the phone. Attackers may impersonate a bank representative, government official, or IT support person to steal personal information.

6. **Smishing (SMS Phishing)**: This involves sending fraudulent text messages designed to trick recipients into clicking malicious links or disclosing sensitive information.

---

**Real-World Examples of Phishing Attacks**

1. **The 2016 Democratic National Committee (DNC) Phishing                        Attack**

   In 2016, **Russian hackers** launched a sophisticated phishing campaign against the **Democratic National Committee (DNC)** during the U.S. presidential election. The attackers sent emails disguised as legitimate communications from Google, asking recipients to change their passwords due to suspicious activity. Once the DNC staff clicked on the links, they were directed to a fake login page that captured their credentials. This attack led to the breach of sensitive emails, which were later leaked and used to influence the election.

   **Outcome**:

   The attack highlighted the effectiveness of **spear-phishing**, a more targeted form of phishing aimed at high-profile individuals. It also emphasized the importance of verifying the authenticity of links before clicking and recognizing the dangers of phishing emails that appear to come from trusted sources.

2. **The 2017 WannaCry Ransomware Attack**
   The **WannaCry ransomware** attack, which spread

globally in 2017, was partially facilitated by phishing emails. The attack used a **phishing email** with an embedded **Excel macro** that tricked users into activating malicious code. Once activated, the ransomware encrypted files and demanded a ransom payment in Bitcoin to restore access.

**Outcome**:

The WannaCry attack affected hundreds of thousands of computers across 150 countries, including healthcare systems like the **UK's National Health Service (NHS)**. The attack demonstrated the potential consequences of phishing and other social engineering tactics, particularly in sectors reliant on outdated software.

3. **The 2011 RSA Breach (The "Pineapple" Phishing Attack)**

   In 2011, **RSA**, a cybersecurity company, was targeted in a phishing attack that led to a significant data breach. The attackers sent an email with an Excel file titled **"2011 Recruitment Plan."** The file contained a malicious exploit that, when opened, allowed the attackers to access sensitive data related to RSA's **SecurID two-factor authentication**

**tokens**. The breach compromised the security of various government and corporate entities, as the stolen information allowed attackers to circumvent multi-factor authentication systems.

**Outcome**:

The breach emphasized the importance of training employees to recognize phishing attempts and the need for robust email security systems, including filtering and scanning attachments.

How to Recognize and Prevent Social Engineering Attacks in the Workplace

Social engineering attacks often rely on human error, making education and vigilance key to preventing them. Here are strategies to recognize and defend against these attacks:

1. **Recognizing Phishing Emails**
   Phishing emails often contain several telltale signs that indicate they are fraudulent:
     - **Suspicious Email Addresses**: Look for slight misspellings in the sender's email

address, such as "@microsofft.com" instead of "@microsoft.com."

- o **Unusual Requests**: Phishing emails often ask for urgent actions, such as providing login credentials, verifying personal information, or clicking on suspicious links.

- o **Generic Greetings**: Phishing emails may use generic phrases like "Dear Customer" rather than addressing you by name.

- o **Attachments and Links**: Be cautious of unsolicited attachments or links. Hover over links to see the actual URL before clicking, and never download attachments from untrusted sources.

2. **Implementing Strong Security Policies**

- o **Multi-Factor Authentication (MFA)**: One of the most effective ways to mitigate the impact of phishing is to require multi-factor authentication for all sensitive accounts. Even if an attacker obtains a password, MFA can prevent unauthorized access.

- o **Regular Software Updates**: Ensure that systems, including email platforms and security software, are regularly updated to protect against known vulnerabilities and exploits.

o **Phishing Simulations**: Many organizations conduct **phishing simulation exercises** to test employee awareness. These exercises involve sending mock phishing emails to employees and measuring how well they can identify potential threats.

3. **Training Employees to Recognize Social Engineering Tactics**

Educating employees is the first line of defense against social engineering attacks. Regular **security awareness training** can help employees identify phishing attempts and understand the risks associated with social engineering. Topics to cover in training include:

o **How to spot phishing emails, fake websites, and phone scams**.

o **How to verify the authenticity of messages** from colleagues, managers, or external contacts.

o **Safe practices for handling sensitive information** and how to report suspicious activity.

4. **Establishing a Reporting Process**
   Employees should know how to report suspicious emails, phone calls, or requests. Having a **clear reporting protocol** ensures that potential threats are escalated quickly to the right security teams for investigation.

5. **Using Advanced Email Filtering and Anti-Phishing Tools**
   Implementing **anti-phishing** and **email filtering** tools can help detect and block phishing emails before they reach the inbox. Tools like **Barracuda**, **Proofpoint**, and **Microsoft Defender for Office 365** can automatically filter out known phishing attempts and malicious attachments.

## Conclusion: The Ongoing Fight Against Social Engineering and Phishing

Social engineering and phishing attacks continue to be among the most successful tactics used by cybercriminals. These attacks prey on human psychology and can have devastating consequences for individuals and organizations alike. However, with the right awareness, training, and security measures in place, the risks associated with these attacks can be significantly reduced.

By recognizing the signs of phishing, educating employees on how to handle sensitive information, and implementing strong security practices, organizations can build a robust defense against social engineering and phishing threats. Ethical hackers and cybersecurity professionals play a vital role in strengthening these defenses and ensuring that companies are prepared to face the ever-evolving threat landscape.

---

This chapter covers the essentials of social engineering and phishing attacks, providing insight into how they work, real-world examples of their impact, and practical steps organizations can take to defend against them.

# CHAPTER 15

# SECURITY OPERATIONS
# CENTERS (SOC)

### Introduction: The Backbone of Cyber Defense

In the rapidly evolving world of cybersecurity, organizations face an ever-growing array of threats, ranging from malicious attacks to internal security breaches. To effectively monitor, detect, and respond to these threats, many organizations establish **Security Operations Centers (SOCs)**. A SOC is a dedicated team and facility responsible for continuously monitoring an organization's security posture, detecting threats, and responding to incidents in real time.

In this chapter, we'll explore the role of SOCs in modern cybersecurity operations, the responsibilities of SOC analysts, and provide real-world examples of how SOC teams respond to security incidents to protect organizations from cyber threats.

**What is a Security Operations Center (SOC)?**

A **Security Operations Center (SOC)** is a centralized unit within an organization that is responsible for monitoring and defending against cybersecurity threats 24/7. It acts as the eyes and ears of an organization's cybersecurity infrastructure, providing continuous monitoring, detection, analysis, and response to security incidents.

**Key Functions of a SOC**:

1. **Threat Monitoring**: The SOC continuously monitors networks, systems, and applications for signs of potential cyber threats, using security tools and technologies to detect anomalies and vulnerabilities.

2. **Incident Detection**: SOCs use automated alerts, threat intelligence feeds, and real-time analysis to identify potential security incidents, such as malware infections, unauthorized access attempts, or data breaches.

3. **Incident Response**: Once a threat is detected, the SOC is responsible for responding to the incident. This can involve containment, eradication,

172

investigation, and recovery actions to minimize damage.

4. **Forensics and Investigation**: In the event of an attack, SOC teams conduct forensic analysis to determine how the attack happened, what systems were affected, and the full scope of the damage.

5. **Threat Intelligence**: SOCs gather and analyze threat intelligence to stay informed about emerging cyber threats and adjust their defenses accordingly.

6. **Reporting and Documentation**: SOCs document all detected incidents, responses, and remediation actions, providing detailed reports to stakeholders and helping organizations comply with regulatory requirements.

**Types of SOCs**:

- **In-House SOC**: Managed internally by an organization's cybersecurity team.
- **Managed SOC (MSSP)**: Outsourced SOC services provided by third-party vendors, often for smaller organizations with limited resources.
- **Hybrid SOC**: A combination of in-house and outsourced SOC resources to provide a flexible approach.

## The Role of SOC Analysts in Monitoring and Defending Against Cyber Threats

SOC analysts are the core of a Security Operations Center. They are responsible for monitoring, detecting, analyzing, and responding to security incidents. Their role is dynamic and requires a combination of technical skills, analytical thinking, and communication to effectively defend against cyber threats.

**Key Responsibilities of SOC Analysts**:

1. **Monitoring Security Alerts**:
   o SOC analysts use a variety of tools such as **SIEM (Security Information and Event Management)** systems to monitor real-time security events and alerts generated by firewalls, intrusion detection/prevention systems (IDS/IPS), endpoint protection platforms, and other security devices.
   o **Example Tools**: **Splunk, Elastic Stack**, and **IBM QRadar** are popular SIEM solutions

174

used by SOC analysts to aggregate logs and identify threats.

2. **Threat Detection and Analysis**:

   o Analysts assess the alerts generated by security tools to identify potential threats, often distinguishing between true positives and false positives. They analyze network traffic, user activity, and system logs to detect signs of attacks, such as **malware infections**, **unauthorized access**, or **data exfiltration**.

   o **Real-Time Monitoring**: SOC analysts need to stay vigilant 24/7 to identify emerging threats like **Zero-Day Exploits**, **botnet activity**, and advanced persistent threats (APTs).

3. **Incident Response and Mitigation**:

   o Once a security incident is detected, SOC analysts are responsible for managing the response. They follow established procedures to contain and mitigate the impact of the incident, including isolating compromised systems, blocking malicious traffic, and preventing further escalation.

- o **Collaboration**: SOC analysts often collaborate with IT, network security teams, and external vendors to remediate the issue and restore normal operations.

4. **Root Cause Analysis**:
   - o After a threat is neutralized, SOC analysts perform a root cause analysis to understand how the attack occurred and what vulnerabilities were exploited. This analysis helps improve defenses and ensures that similar attacks do not happen in the future.

5. **Reporting and Documentation**:
   - o SOC analysts document their findings and response actions in detailed reports for management, legal teams, and regulatory bodies. These reports may be required for compliance purposes and provide insights for improving security posture.

**SOC Analyst Levels**:

- **Tier 1 (Entry-Level)**: Responsible for monitoring alerts, triaging incidents, and escalating issues to higher-level analysts.

- **Tier 2 (Intermediate)**: Focus on investigating and analyzing incidents, identifying potential attacks, and providing remediation recommendations.
- **Tier 3 (Advanced)**: Handles complex incidents, conducts deep forensics and malware analysis, and may provide threat-hunting services.

## Real-World Examples of How SOC Teams Respond to Security Incidents

1. **The Target Data Breach (2013)**
   The **Target** data breach is a widely known example of how a SOC can respond to an incident. Attackers used **phishing emails** to gain access to Target's network, eventually compromising payment card information from millions of customers. Once the breach was detected, Target's SOC team worked quickly to contain the attack, investigate the scope of the data theft, and begin remediation efforts.

   **SOC Actions**:

- o Target's SOC analyzed network traffic and logs to identify how the attackers gained access.
- o The team isolated affected systems and began the process of removing the malware from the network.
- o Target worked with external forensics experts to determine the full scope of the breach, including how the attackers gained access and which data was exfiltrated.

**Outcome**:

After the breach, Target enhanced its cybersecurity measures by implementing stronger network segmentation, improving vendor management processes, and rolling out chip-enabled credit cards to reduce the risk of future attacks.

2. **The WannaCry Ransomware Attack (2017)**
The **WannaCry** ransomware attack in 2017 exploited a vulnerability in **Microsoft Windows** systems, affecting hundreds of thousands of computers worldwide. Organizations such as the **UK's National Health Service (NHS)** were among

the hardest hit. The attack was rapidly detected and mitigated by SOC teams around the world.

**SOC Actions**:

- SOC teams used network monitoring tools to detect abnormal file encryption behavior indicative of the ransomware attack.
- Analysts quickly identified the exploited **EternalBlue** vulnerability and began applying patches to vulnerable systems across organizations.
- SOCs worked with incident response teams to isolate affected machines, block the ransomware's propagation, and prevent further data encryption.

**Outcome**:

The WannaCry attack underscored the importance of timely patching and regular vulnerability management. Organizations that had already applied the Microsoft patch were able to avoid significant damage, while others faced massive disruptions to operations.

3. **The SolarWinds Supply Chain Attack (2020)**

   The **SolarWinds** attack involved a sophisticated supply chain attack that compromised the **SolarWinds Orion software** updates, which were used by thousands of organizations, including government agencies and large enterprises. The attackers inserted a backdoor into the software, giving them remote access to the networks of affected organizations.

   **SOC Actions**:

   - SOC teams continuously monitored network traffic and user behavior for signs of abnormal activity related to the SolarWinds backdoor.
   - The SolarWinds attack was eventually detected by **FireEye's** SOC team, who noticed unusual behavior within their own network and traced it back to the compromised Orion updates.
   - Affected organizations worked with the SOC to remove the malicious code, apply patches, and improve their network monitoring practices.

**Outcome**:

The SolarWinds breach highlighted the vulnerability of supply chains and the need for robust monitoring of third-party software. SOCs enhanced their focus on **threat-hunting** and **supply chain security** to protect against similar attacks in the future.

---

**Conclusion: The Critical Role of SOCs in Cybersecurity**

Security Operations Centers (SOCs) are essential for defending organizations against the growing number of cyber threats. By providing continuous monitoring, real-time threat detection, and incident response, SOC teams ensure that vulnerabilities are identified and mitigated before they can be exploited by cybercriminals. From handling basic security alerts to managing complex incidents, SOC analysts play a vital role in maintaining the security and integrity of an organization's systems.

As cyber threats continue to evolve, SOCs must adapt, incorporating new technologies, threat intelligence, and proactive strategies to stay ahead of attackers. Organizations that invest in well-structured SOCs and prioritize the continuous training of their analysts are better equipped to navigate the ever-changing cybersecurity landscape.

---

This chapter provides an in-depth look at the role of Security Operations Centers (SOCs) and how they defend against cyber threats. Let me know if you would like further details on any of the topics or examples!

# CHAPTER 16

# INCIDENT RESPONSE: HOW TO HANDLE A BREACH

### Introduction: The Importance of Incident Response

When a cybersecurity breach occurs, it can feel like chaos. Systems may be compromised, data may be stolen, and the integrity of the organization's infrastructure may be at risk. In the midst of a breach, the ability to respond quickly, efficiently, and systematically is critical. This is where **incident response (IR)** comes into play.

**Incident response** refers to the structured approach taken by organizations to detect, respond to, and recover from cybersecurity incidents. A well-defined incident response plan (IRP) helps organizations contain the damage, minimize data loss, and ensure business continuity. In this chapter, we'll break down the steps of incident response, explore what happens when a breach occurs, and examine real-world case studies of organizations effectively managing cybersecurity incidents.

## What Happens When a Breach Occurs?

When a cybersecurity breach happens, an organization faces immediate challenges. A breach could be the result of a **hacker intrusion**, **malware infection**, **data leak**, or a **denial-of-service (DoS) attack**. Regardless of the cause, the organization needs to act quickly to limit the damage and restore operations.

**Key Questions to Address**:

- **What systems or data have been compromised?** Understanding the scope of the breach is critical to managing the incident and protecting sensitive data.
- **How did the attackers gain access?** Identifying the entry point helps determine how to close the security gaps and prevent similar breaches in the future.
- **What immediate steps need to be taken to contain the damage?** Immediate containment actions, such as isolating affected systems or blocking malicious IP addresses, are necessary to prevent the spread of the attack.

- **How can we communicate with stakeholders, employees, and the public?** Communication is crucial during a breach to maintain transparency and trust with customers, partners, and regulatory bodies.

A breach typically triggers the organization's incident response plan, which outlines the necessary steps and assigns responsibilities to specific teams.

---

**The Steps of Incident Response: Identification, Containment, Eradication, Recovery**

Incident response follows a structured process to ensure that the breach is handled methodically. The process can be broken down into four main phases: **Identification**, **Containment**, **Eradication**, and **Recovery**.

*1. Identification*

**Identification** is the first step of incident response and involves detecting that a security breach has occurred. This step is crucial because prompt detection allows for quicker response times, minimizing damage.

**Actions during the Identification phase**:

- **Monitor for anomalies**: Continuously monitor network traffic, system logs, and user behavior to identify signs of a breach.

- **Analyze security alerts**: Use **SIEM (Security Information and Event Management)** tools and other monitoring platforms to analyze logs and identify suspicious activity.

- **Verify the breach**: Once an alert is generated, the IR team must confirm that a breach has actually occurred and determine the scope of the incident (e.g., is it an isolated event or a widespread attack?).

**Real-World                                    Example**:

In 2017, **Equifax** suffered a major breach where hackers exploited a vulnerability in a web application framework. The breach wasn't detected for several weeks, highlighting the importance of timely identification of vulnerabilities. If identification had been faster, the breach might have been mitigated sooner.

## 2. Containment

**Containment** involves taking immediate steps to limit the impact of the breach by preventing further spread or access. During this phase, it is essential to isolate the affected systems while keeping the business running.

**Actions during the Containment phase**:

- **Isolate compromised systems**: Disconnect affected systems from the network to prevent further damage and data exfiltration.
- **Implement temporary fixes**: Use **firewalls, intrusion detection systems (IDS)**, and **endpoint protection** to block additional attacks or access.
- **Monitor for lateral movement**: Ensure that attackers cannot move through the network to other vulnerable systems.

**Real-World                                        Example**: During the **NotPetya ransomware attack** (2017), companies that were affected, such as **Maersk**, took immediate containment actions by isolating infected machines. This step helped prevent the spread of the ransomware across the company's network, although recovery was still a lengthy process.

*3. Eradication*

After containment, the next phase is **eradication**, where the goal is to completely remove the malicious elements from the environment. This includes deleting malware, closing vulnerabilities, and ensuring that no traces of the breach remain.

**Actions during the Eradication phase**:

- **Remove malicious software**: Use antivirus tools, malware scanners, and manual cleanup techniques to ensure that all traces of the malware or attack are gone.
- **Patch vulnerabilities**: Apply security patches or configuration changes to fix the vulnerabilities that were exploited during the attack.
- **Restore compromised credentials**: If credentials were stolen, reset passwords and implement multi-factor authentication (MFA) to secure accounts.

**Real-World                                    Example**:
In the **Sony Pictures Entertainment hack** (2014), after the

breach was contained, the company took steps to completely eradicate the malicious malware that had been installed on its systems. This included rebuilding the compromised network, removing backdoors, and resetting employee credentials.

## 4. Recovery

**Recovery** is the final phase of incident response, where the organization works to restore systems to normal operations. This phase can involve rebuilding damaged systems, testing for vulnerabilities, and ensuring that security controls are in place to prevent future incidents.

**Actions during the Recovery phase**:

- **Restore from backups**: If necessary, restore lost data from **secure backups** and ensure that it has not been compromised.
- **Test systems for integrity**: Conduct tests to verify that the restored systems are secure and free from any traces of the attack.
- **Communicate with stakeholders**: Keep employees, customers, regulators, and the public informed about

the breach and what steps are being taken to prevent future incidents.

**Real-World** **Example**: After the **WannaCry ransomware attack**, affected organizations like the **NHS (National Health Service)** worked to recover their systems by applying the Microsoft patch that would have prevented the attack and restoring critical services from backups. Recovery was a lengthy process but was made easier by the proactive application of patches and a strong backup system.

---

## Case Studies of Organizations Handling Cybersecurity Incidents

*1. The 2013 Target Data Breach*

In 2013, **Target** experienced a massive data breach that compromised the personal and financial information of over **40 million customers**. The breach began with a phishing attack that targeted a third-party vendor, which gave attackers access to Target's network.

**Incident Response Actions**:

- **Identification**: The breach was identified after suspicious activity was detected by Target's network monitoring tools.
- **Containment**: The company quickly isolated the affected systems and initiated a process to remove malware from its network.
- **Eradication**: The compromised network segments were secured, and Target implemented better segmentation to prevent future attacks.
- **Recovery**: Target worked to notify affected customers, offer credit monitoring, and rebuild trust with its customer base.

**Outcome**:

The breach cost Target over **$200 million** in direct expenses, including legal costs and compensation. However, the company learned valuable lessons in cybersecurity, strengthening vendor management and implementing improved network monitoring and encryption practices.

*2. The 2017 WannaCry Ransomware Attack*

The **WannaCry ransomware** attack in 2017 impacted over **200,000 computers** across 150 countries. It exploited a vulnerability in the **Microsoft Windows SMB protocol**, causing widespread disruption, especially in healthcare systems.

**Incident Response Actions**:

- **Identification**: The attack was identified by researchers after it spread rapidly across networks, encrypting files and demanding a ransom in Bitcoin.
- **Containment**: Organizations immediately isolated infected machines to prevent further spread of the ransomware.
- **Eradication**: Microsoft issued a security patch to close the exploited vulnerability, and affected systems were cleaned of the ransomware.
- **Recovery**: Organizations restored systems from backups and applied the latest security patches to ensure that systems were secure.

**Outcome**:

The WannaCry attack highlighted the critical importance of **patch management** and regular software updates. Organizations that had applied the necessary patches were able to avoid the attack, while those that had not faced significant disruption.

## Conclusion: The Critical Role of Incident Response

Incident response is a crucial part of an organization's cybersecurity strategy. A well-prepared incident response plan allows organizations to quickly identify, contain, and recover from security incidents, minimizing damage and ensuring that they can continue operations as smoothly as possible. The ability to learn from past incidents and continuously improve processes is key to building resilience in an increasingly complex threat landscape.

By following the structured phases of **identification**, **containment**, **eradication**, and **recovery**, organizations can reduce the impact of a breach and strengthen their security posture for the future.

This chapter provides an overview of how organizations handle cybersecurity breaches, detailing the steps involved in incident response and providing real-world case studies of organizations effectively managing cybersecurity incidents.

# *CHAPTER 17*

# *RISK MANAGEMENT IN CYBERSECURITY*

## Introduction: The Critical Role of Risk Management in Cybersecurity

Cybersecurity risks are an ever-present concern for organizations of all sizes. These risks can take many forms: from data breaches and insider threats to ransomware and advanced persistent threats (APTs). In order to effectively safeguard sensitive information and maintain business operations, organizations must adopt a systematic approach to identifying, evaluating, and mitigating cybersecurity risks. This approach is known as **risk management**.

In this chapter, we will explore the core concepts of **risk assessment** and **risk management**, discuss how to identify, evaluate, and mitigate risks, and provide real-world examples of effective risk management strategies.

---

## Understanding Risk Assessment and Risk Management

## 1. What is Risk Assessment?

**Risk assessment** is the process of identifying and analyzing potential risks that could impact an organization's cybersecurity. The goal is to understand the likelihood and impact of various risks so that appropriate measures can be taken to mitigate them.

**Key Components of Risk Assessment**:

- **Asset Identification**: Identify valuable assets that need protection (e.g., data, systems, intellectual property).
- **Threat Identification**: Identify potential threats, such as hackers, malware, human error, or natural disasters.
- **Vulnerability Identification**: Identify weaknesses or vulnerabilities in the system that could be exploited by threats (e.g., unpatched software, weak passwords).
- **Impact Analysis**: Evaluate the potential consequences of a successful attack (e.g., financial loss, reputational damage, legal consequences).

- **Likelihood Assessment**: Estimate the likelihood that a threat will exploit a vulnerability and cause harm to the organization.

**Risk Assessment Methodology**:

1. **Qualitative Assessment**: Involves subjective evaluation of risks based on experience and judgment. Risks are typically rated as high, medium, or low.
2. **Quantitative Assessment**: Involves the use of data and metrics to calculate the probability and financial impact of risks. This is often used in industries where financial loss can be precisely quantified.
3. **What is Risk Management?**

**Risk management** is the process of identifying, evaluating, and taking steps to minimize or eliminate risks that could potentially affect an organization. It's a holistic approach to ensuring that an organization is not only aware of potential risks but also prepared to respond to and mitigate them.

**Key Components of Risk Management**:

- **Risk Identification**: The first step is identifying all potential risks that could affect the organization, which involves assessing both external and internal threats.

- **Risk Evaluation**: Once identified, risks need to be evaluated based on their potential impact and the likelihood of them occurring.

- **Risk Mitigation**: Implement strategies to reduce or eliminate the impact of the risks. This could include **technical controls** (e.g., firewalls, encryption), **operational controls** (e.g., employee training, access management), and **physical controls** (e.g., data center security).

- **Risk Monitoring and Review**: Ongoing monitoring and periodic review of risk management efforts ensure that new risks are identified, and mitigation strategies are working as expected.

**Risk Management Strategies**:

- **Risk Avoidance**: Taking actions to eliminate the risk altogether, such as avoiding certain activities or moving operations to a safer environment.

- **Risk Reduction**: Implementing controls to reduce the likelihood or impact of a risk (e.g., using encryption to protect sensitive data).

- **Risk Sharing**: Transferring the risk to a third party, such as purchasing cybersecurity insurance or outsourcing to a managed service provider.
- **Risk Acceptance**: In some cases, an organization may decide to accept the risk if the potential impact is deemed low or if mitigating the risk is too costly.

## How to Identify, Evaluate, and Mitigate Cybersecurity Risks

### 1. Identifying Cybersecurity Risks

The first step in risk management is identifying the cybersecurity risks an organization faces. These can be internal (e.g., employees, weak passwords) or external (e.g., cybercriminals, supply chain vulnerabilities). Common methods for identifying cybersecurity risks include:

- **Risk Workshops and Brainstorming**: Bringing together key stakeholders, such as IT staff, security teams, and management, to identify potential risks.
- **Vulnerability Scanning**: Using automated tools to scan systems for known vulnerabilities.

- **Penetration Testing**: Conducting ethical hacking exercises to identify weaknesses in systems and networks.
- **Third-Party Assessments**: Collaborating with external experts to assess vulnerabilities and risks from a fresh perspective.

2. **Evaluating Cybersecurity Risks**

Once risks are identified, the next step is to evaluate them based on two factors:

- **Likelihood**: How likely is it that the identified risk will occur? This can be based on historical data, threat intelligence, or expert judgment.
- **Impact**: What would be the impact on the organization if the risk were to occur? The impact can be financial, reputational, legal, or operational.

Risk evaluation tools and techniques:

- **Risk Matrices**: A risk matrix is a graphical tool that plots the likelihood of a risk against its potential impact, helping prioritize risks based on their severity.

- **Business Impact Analysis (BIA)**: A BIA helps assess how critical each business function is and the impact of losing or disrupting that function due to a risk event.

3. **Mitigating Cybersecurity Risks**

Once risks have been identified and evaluated, organizations can implement strategies to mitigate them. Common risk mitigation strategies include:

- **Implementing Technical Controls**: Deploying **firewalls**, **intrusion detection systems (IDS)**, **data encryption**, **access control mechanisms**, and other tools to reduce exposure to threats.
- **Employee Training**: Educating employees on best practices for cybersecurity, such as recognizing phishing emails, securing passwords, and following secure protocols.
- **Patch Management**: Regularly applying security patches and updates to software and hardware to close vulnerabilities before attackers can exploit them.
- **Incident Response Planning**: Developing and testing an incident response plan so that the

200

organization can respond quickly and effectively to security breaches.

---

**Real-World Examples of Risk Management Strategies**

1. **The Equifax Data Breach (2017)**
   The **Equifax** data breach was a massive incident in which sensitive data, including personal details and Social Security numbers of over **147 million Americans**, were stolen. The breach was caused by the exploitation of a known vulnerability in the **Apache Struts** web application framework that Equifax had failed to patch.

   **Risk Management Failures**:

   o **Failure to Patch Vulnerabilities**: Equifax did not apply a security patch for the vulnerability in time, which led to the breach.
   o **Inadequate Monitoring**: The attack went undetected for months, highlighting weaknesses in Equifax's ability to monitor for intrusions.

**Post-Incident Risk Management**:

- o After the breach, Equifax implemented a more robust patch management system and improved its monitoring and detection capabilities. The company also offered credit monitoring services to affected customers and worked on rebuilding trust.

2. **The 2017 WannaCry Ransomware Attack**
The **WannaCry ransomware** attack targeted organizations worldwide, exploiting a Windows vulnerability that had been patched by Microsoft months before the attack. The rapid spread of WannaCry caused significant disruptions to systems, including the **UK National Health Service (NHS)**.

**Risk Management Strategy**:

- o **Patch Management**: Many organizations that applied the security patch issued by Microsoft before the attack were not affected. The breach highlighted the critical importance of patching systems promptly.
- o **Backup and Recovery Plans**: Affected organizations that had regular data backups

were able to recover quickly without paying the ransom.

**Post-Incident Risk Management**:

- o After WannaCry, organizations adopted stronger patch management protocols, implemented more frequent backups, and began using **network segmentation** to limit the spread of malware.

3. **The Target Data Breach (2013)**
The Target data breach was caused by attackers who used **phishing emails** to steal credentials from a third-party vendor. They then used the compromised credentials to access Target's internal network, stealing credit card information from millions of customers.

**Risk Management Failures**:

- o **Third-Party Vendor Risk**: Target's third-party vendor was compromised, highlighting the need for stronger controls over third-party vendors.

o **Lack of Network Segmentation**: Once inside the network, the attackers were able to move freely and access sensitive data.

**Post-Incident Risk Management**:

o Target enhanced its vendor risk management policies and implemented stronger network segmentation to prevent future breaches. They also introduced **multi-factor authentication (MFA)** to secure access to sensitive systems.

---

## Conclusion: The Ongoing Journey of Risk Management

Cybersecurity risk management is not a one-time activity but an ongoing process that requires continuous monitoring, evaluation, and adaptation. As the threat landscape evolves, so too must an organization's risk management strategies. A proactive and comprehensive approach to identifying, evaluating, and mitigating risks can help organizations reduce vulnerabilities, protect critical data, and maintain the trust of customers and stakeholders.

By learning from real-world examples of cyber incidents and implementing robust risk management strategies, organizations can enhance their ability to respond to cybersecurity threats and build resilience in the face of future risks.

---

This chapter provides an overview of the importance of risk management in cybersecurity, the steps involved in assessing and mitigating risks, and examples of how organizations have successfully applied risk management strategies.

# CHAPTER 18

# THE ROLE OF AUTOMATION AND AI IN CYBERSECURITY

## Introduction: The Changing Landscape of Cybersecurity

In today's fast-paced and constantly evolving cyber threat landscape, traditional methods of cybersecurity are increasingly inadequate. Attackers are becoming more sophisticated, leveraging advanced tools and tactics that require rapid detection and response. To keep up with these challenges, cybersecurity professionals are turning to **automation** and **artificial intelligence (AI)** to enhance their defenses. These technologies are transforming the way cybersecurity is managed, from threat detection to incident response, and are playing a crucial role in helping organizations proactively defend against cyberattacks.

In this chapter, we'll explore how automation and AI are reshaping cybersecurity, provide examples of AI-driven tools for threat detection and analysis, and discuss the future of automation in cybersecurity and its impact on job roles.

206

# How Automation and AI Are Transforming Cybersecurity

1. **The Role of Automation in Cybersecurity**

   **Automation** in cybersecurity refers to the use of technology to perform repetitive tasks or processes without human intervention. These tasks can include monitoring network traffic, applying security patches, or responding to known threats. Automation helps streamline cybersecurity processes, reduce human error, and enable faster detection and remediation of security incidents.

   **Key Benefits of Automation**:

   o **Speed**: Automated systems can respond to threats much faster than human teams, reducing the time it takes to detect and mitigate potential attacks.

   o **Consistency**: Automation ensures that tasks are performed consistently, reducing the likelihood of human error and ensuring compliance with security protocols.

○ **Efficiency**: Automation allows security teams to focus on higher-level tasks, such as strategy development and incident investigation, by handling routine, time-consuming tasks automatically.

**Examples of Automation in Cybersecurity**:

○ **Automated Patch Management**: Security tools can automatically apply patches to known vulnerabilities across an organization's systems without requiring manual intervention.

○ **Incident Response Automation**: Security automation platforms can automatically respond to security incidents, such as blocking IP addresses or isolating affected systems, based on predefined rules.

2. **The Role of AI in Cybersecurity**
**Artificial intelligence (AI)** refers to systems that can perform tasks that would typically require human intelligence, such as learning, problem-solving, and decision-making. In cybersecurity, AI is being used to detect, analyze, and respond to threats with greater accuracy and efficiency than traditional methods.

**Key Benefits of AI in Cybersecurity**:

- ○ **Threat Detection and Prediction**: AI can analyze vast amounts of data to identify patterns and detect potential threats, such as zero-day attacks or advanced persistent threats (APTs), that might go unnoticed by traditional security systems.

- ○ **Behavioral Analytics**: AI systems can monitor user behavior and network activity to identify deviations from the norm, such as unusual login times or unauthorized data access, which could indicate a breach.

- ○ **Adaptive Defense**: AI-powered systems can learn from past incidents, continuously improving their ability to detect new threats and respond appropriately.

**Examples of AI in Cybersecurity**:

- ○ **AI-driven Intrusion Detection Systems (IDS)**: AI-based IDS can analyze network traffic in real-time to identify potential intrusions, flagging suspicious activity and providing security teams with actionable insights.

- o **AI-powered Security Information and Event Management (SIEM)**: SIEM systems that incorporate AI use machine learning algorithms to analyze logs, detect anomalies, and provide contextualized alerts, improving the accuracy of threat detection.

- o **AI-based Malware Detection**: AI systems can be trained to recognize patterns in malware behavior, helping identify new strains of malware before they cause significant damage.

## Examples of AI-Driven Tools for Threat Detection and Analysis

1. **Darktrace**

   **Darktrace** is an AI-driven cybersecurity platform that uses machine learning and **unsupervised learning** to detect and respond to cyber threats in real time. It uses AI to analyze network traffic and identify abnormal behavior, such as unauthorized access or data exfiltration. Darktrace's **Enterprise Immune System** mimics the human immune system by learning the normal "patterns of life" for users, devices, and applications and then detecting deviations from those patterns.

**Key Features**:

- o **Autonomous Response**: Darktrace can automatically take actions to contain or mitigate threats without requiring manual intervention.
- o **AI-Powered Anomaly Detection**: The system uses AI to detect previously unknown or zero-day attacks based on abnormal behavior rather than relying on known signatures.
- o **Real-Time Threat Detection**: Darktrace provides real-time visibility into network traffic and alerts security teams about potential threats.

2. **CrowdStrike**

**CrowdStrike** is a cloud-delivered endpoint protection platform that uses AI and machine learning to protect against cyberattacks. Its **Falcon**

211

platform leverages AI to detect threats, investigate incidents, and respond in real-time. It is widely used for detecting malware, ransomware, and advanced threats on endpoints.

**Key Features**:

- o **AI-Powered Threat Hunting**: CrowdStrike uses machine learning to detect and block threats on endpoints, even those that are previously unknown or not yet identified by traditional antivirus software.
- o **Real-Time Behavioral Analysis**: Falcon analyzes system behavior and correlates data from multiple endpoints to identify attack patterns and unusual activities.
- o **Incident Response**: CrowdStrike provides automated incident response, enabling rapid containment and remediation.

3. **Vectra** **AI**

**Vectra AI** specializes in **network detection and response (NDR)**. It uses AI to monitor and analyze network traffic to detect cyberattacks in real time. Vectra focuses on using AI to identify **lateral movement, data exfiltration**, and other indicators of compromise within the network, often before traditional defenses can detect them.

**Key Features**:

- o **AI-Powered Threat Detection**: Vectra AI uses machine learning to detect malicious activity and identify complex attacks that evade traditional security measures.
- o **Automated Incident Response**: Vectra can automate response actions based on detected threats, helping to stop attacks in their tracks.
- o **Contextual Alerts**: The platform provides detailed context around alerts, allowing security teams to prioritize incidents based on severity and impact.

---

**The Future of Automation in Cybersecurity and Its Impact on Job Roles**

1. **The Growing Role of Automation and AI in Cybersecurity**

   As cyber threats continue to evolve, the role of **automation** and **AI** in cybersecurity will expand significantly. These technologies will increasingly take on routine and repetitive tasks, such as monitoring logs, scanning for vulnerabilities, and responding to known threats. This will allow cybersecurity professionals to focus on more strategic activities, such as threat hunting, incident analysis, and policy development.

**Future Trends**:

- o **AI for Proactive Threat Hunting**: AI will enable more proactive cybersecurity measures by identifying threats before they can escalate into full-fledged attacks.
- o **Automated Remediation**: In the future, AI and automation will not only detect and respond to threats but also take corrective actions, such as patching vulnerabilities and isolating infected systems.
- o **Advanced Predictive Capabilities**: AI will evolve to predict and mitigate attacks based on patterns and emerging threats, allowing organizations to get ahead of cybercriminals.

2. **Impact on Job Roles**
While AI and automation will enhance the

214

capabilities of cybersecurity teams, they will also have an impact on job roles within the industry.

**Job Role Changes**:

- o **Shift in Skill Sets**: Traditional roles such as **network administrators** and **system analysts** will evolve. Cybersecurity professionals will need to acquire skills in AI, machine learning, and data science to work effectively with automated systems and AI-driven tools.

- o **Increased Focus on Strategic Roles**: As automation takes care of routine tasks, cybersecurity professionals will increasingly focus on higher-level responsibilities, such as strategy, risk management, and governance.

- o **Job Creation in AI and Automation**: New roles will emerge in AI and automation management, such as **AI Security Analysts** and **Automation Engineers**, who will design, implement, and optimize these technologies.

**Real-World** **Example**:

In the financial sector, AI and automation are already transforming roles in **fraud detection**. Traditionally, fraud detection involved manual analysis of transactions, but AI-driven systems now handle this task, flagging suspicious activity in real-time and reducing false positives. This shift has led to a demand for cybersecurity professionals who specialize in AI and machine learning techniques to improve these automated systems.

## Conclusion: The Future of Cybersecurity Powered by AI and Automation

The integration of **automation** and **AI** into cybersecurity is not just a trend—it's a necessity in today's threat landscape. These technologies are transforming the way organizations detect, respond to, and mitigate cybersecurity threats, offering faster, more accurate, and scalable solutions. While automation and AI are improving efficiency and effectiveness, they also require cybersecurity professionals to adapt to new roles and develop skills that align with the evolving digital landscape.

The future of cybersecurity will be one where automation and AI not only enhance the human element of defense but also redefine how security teams operate, allowing them to proactively protect organizations from the ever-growing array of cyber threats.

This chapter covers the role of automation and AI in transforming cybersecurity, the tools that are being developed to improve threat detection and response, and how these changes will impact job roles in the future.

## *CHAPTER 19*

## *CYBERSECURITY CERTIFICATIONS: WHICH ONES SHOULD YOU PURSUE?*

### Introduction: The Power of Cybersecurity Certifications

In the competitive field of cybersecurity, **certifications** are a powerful tool for demonstrating your expertise, improving your skills, and enhancing your career prospects. With the increasing number of cyber threats, organizations need professionals with verified knowledge and skills to protect their systems and data. Earning cybersecurity certifications not only proves your capabilities but also signals your commitment to professional development.

This chapter will provide an overview of key cybersecurity certifications such as **CompTIA Security+**, **Certified Ethical Hacker (CEH)**, **Certified Information Systems Security Professional (CISSP)**, and **Certified Information Security Manager (CISM)**. We will also explore how these certifications can advance your career and share real-world stories of professionals who leveraged their certifications to achieve career success.

## Overview of Key Cybersecurity Certifications

1.  **CompTIA Security+**

    **CompTIA Security+** is one of the most well-known entry-level certifications in cybersecurity. It covers a broad range of security topics, making it an excellent starting point for those new to the field. The certification focuses on essential security concepts such as risk management, network security, encryption, identity management, and incident response.

    **Why You Should Pursue It**:

    - o **Widely Recognized**: Security+ is a foundational certification that is recognized by employers worldwide.
    - o **Entry-Level Friendly**: It's ideal for individuals who are new to cybersecurity, as it does not require extensive experience.

- o **Comprehensive Coverage**: The certification provides a strong understanding of the core concepts necessary for any cybersecurity role.

**Exam Topics**:

- o Threats, attacks, and vulnerabilities
- o Identity and access management
- o Network security
- o Cryptography and public key infrastructure (PKI)
- o Risk management and compliance

**Real-World Example**: **John**, a recent college graduate with a degree in information technology, was struggling to break into the cybersecurity industry. After earning the **CompTIA Security+** certification, he landed a position as a **security analyst**. The certification gave him the credibility and foundational knowledge needed to start his career in cybersecurity.

2. **Certified Ethical Hacker (CEH)**

**Certified Ethical Hacker (CEH)** is a certification for professionals who want to pursue a career in ethical hacking and penetration testing. CEH focuses on the tools and techniques used by malicious hackers, teaching you how to think like a hacker in order to defend against attacks.

**Why You Should Pursue It**:

- o **Specialized Knowledge**: It's ideal for professionals who want to specialize in penetration testing and ethical hacking.
- o **Hands-On Learning**: The certification teaches practical skills in hacking techniques, vulnerability assessments, and exploiting weaknesses in networks and systems.
- o **Industry Demand**: Ethical hackers are in high demand as organizations seek to identify and fix vulnerabilities before malicious hackers can exploit them.

**Exam Topics**:

- o Footprinting and reconnaissance
- o Scanning networks and enumeration

221

- o System hacking
- o Malware threats
- o Web application vulnerabilities

**Real-World Example**: **Sara**, a junior network administrator, wanted to switch to a more challenging and specialized role. After earning her **CEH** certification, she was hired as a **penetration tester** at a cybersecurity consulting firm. The hands-on skills she gained from the certification helped her land the job and excel in her new career.

3. **Certified Information Systems Security Professional (CISSP)**

**CISSP** is one of the most prestigious and recognized certifications for cybersecurity professionals. It is designed for experienced security practitioners and focuses on the management of information security programs. CISSP is ideal for professionals aiming for managerial roles such as **security architect**, **chief information security officer (CISO)**, or **security consultant**.

**Why You Should Pursue It:**

- o **Advanced Certification**: CISSP is an advanced certification, requiring a minimum of five years of professional experience in the information security field.
- o **Globally Recognized**: CISSP is considered a gold standard in cybersecurity and is often required for high-level security positions.
- o **Broader Scope**: CISSP covers a wide range of topics, including risk management, security architecture, and governance, making it ideal for those interested in managerial roles.

**Exam Topics**:

- o Security and risk management
- o Asset security
- o Security engineering
- o Communication and network security
- o Identity and access management
- o Security operations

**Real-World Example**: **Mike**, a senior security analyst with several years of experience, earned the **CISSP** certification to move into a leadership role.

223

After obtaining the certification, Mike transitioned into a **security architect** position, where he now designs and implements security frameworks for large corporations. The CISSP certification was instrumental in helping him advance in his career.

4. **Certified Information Security Manager (CISM)**

**CISM** is a certification that focuses on the management and governance aspects of cybersecurity. It is designed for professionals who are responsible for managing, designing, and assessing an organization's information security program. CISM is ideal for those who want to move into security management or leadership roles.

**Why You Should Pursue It**:

o **Focus on Security Management**: CISM is tailored for individuals interested in managing security programs, risk management, and organizational security governance.

- o **Leadership Roles**: CISM prepares professionals for leadership roles, such as **information security manager** or **CISO**.
- o **Proven Expertise**: Organizations recognize CISM as a symbol of a comprehensive understanding of cybersecurity management.

**Exam Topics**:

- o Information security governance
- o Information risk management
- o Information security program development
- o Incident response and recovery

**Real-World Example**: **Emily**, who had been working as an IT security professional for years, decided to pursue **CISM** to transition into a management position. After obtaining her CISM certification, Emily was promoted to **information security manager** at a large financial institution, where she now oversees the company's entire security program.

---

**How Certifications Can Boost Your Career Prospects**

Cybersecurity certifications provide several career advantages, including:

- **Credibility**: Certifications validate your expertise and demonstrate your commitment to staying updated on the latest security trends and technologies.
- **Better Job Opportunities**: Many cybersecurity positions, particularly those at senior levels, require certifications. Having the right credentials can help you stand out in a competitive job market.
- **Higher Salary**: Cybersecurity professionals with certifications tend to earn higher salaries than those without. For example, professionals with CISSP certification can earn 20-30% more than their non-certified peers.
- **Professional Growth**: Certifications often lead to job promotions or career transitions by equipping you with the necessary skills and knowledge for advanced roles in cybersecurity.

---

**Real-World Stories of Professionals Advancing Their Careers Through Certifications**

1. **Jason's Journey from Network Administrator to CISO**

   Jason started his career as a network administrator but found himself wanting to move into higher-level security management roles. After earning his **CISSP** certification, he transitioned to a security architect position, where he developed security strategies for large enterprise systems. Within two years, Jason's expertise and CISSP certification helped him secure the position of **Chief Information Security Officer (CISO)** at a major corporation.

2. **Tina's Success in Ethical Hacking**

   Tina was working as a junior systems administrator and was eager to explore ethical hacking. She decided to pursue the **CEH** certification, which provided her with hands-on experience and knowledge in penetration testing and ethical hacking. With her new skill set, Tina moved into a penetration tester role and later became a lead consultant for a cybersecurity firm specializing in vulnerability assessments and ethical hacking.

3. **Mark's Career Growth with Security+**

   Mark was an entry-level IT support technician with an interest in cybersecurity. After obtaining the

227

**CompTIA Security+** certification, Mark was promoted to a **security analyst** position. He continued to expand his knowledge with additional certifications, ultimately advancing into a **security engineer** role where he designs security infrastructure for a large tech company.

---

## Conclusion: Choosing the Right Certification for Your Cybersecurity Career

Cybersecurity certifications are a powerful way to enhance your career and validate your skills in the ever-growing field of cybersecurity. Whether you are just starting out or looking to advance into a leadership role, certifications like **CompTIA Security+**, **CEH**, **CISSP**, and **CISM** can provide you with the knowledge, credibility, and career opportunities you need. By investing in certifications, you are investing in your professional growth and increasing your chances of success in the rapidly evolving cybersecurity landscape.

This chapter provided an overview of the most important cybersecurity certifications and how they can boost your career prospects.

# CHAPTER 20

# BUILDING A STRONG CYBERSECURITY PORTFOLIO

## Introduction: The Importance of a Cybersecurity Portfolio

In today's competitive job market, a well-crafted **cybersecurity portfolio** can be your ticket to landing your first job in cybersecurity. While certifications, experience, and education are all critical, a portfolio allows you to showcase your hands-on skills, real-world problem-solving abilities, and passion for the field. A strong portfolio demonstrates that you can apply your knowledge to actual cybersecurity challenges, making you stand out to potential employers.

In this chapter, we'll explore how to create a compelling cybersecurity portfolio, highlight how to demonstrate your skills with real-world projects and experiences, and provide case studies of successful portfolios that helped professionals land their jobs in cybersecurity.

# How to Create a Compelling Portfolio to Land Your First Job

1. **Start with the Basics: Resume and Cover Letter**

   Before you build your portfolio, make sure your **resume** and **cover letter** are in order. These documents are often the first impression employers have of you, so they should effectively communicate your skills, certifications, and experience.

   - **Resume Tips**: Focus on your cybersecurity skills, certifications (e.g., **CompTIA Security+**, **CEH**, etc.), and any related projects, internships, or volunteer work.
   - **Cover Letter Tips**: Tailor your cover letter to each job application, explaining why you are passionate about cybersecurity, what skills you bring to the role, and how you can contribute to the organization's security needs.

2. **Showcase Hands-On Projects**

231

One of the most effective ways to demonstrate your skills is by showcasing **hands-on projects**. These projects not only allow you to apply your theoretical knowledge but also give potential employers concrete evidence of your abilities. If you are just starting in cybersecurity, here are some project ideas to help build your portfolio:

- o **Network Security Projects**: Set up your own network and implement basic security measures such as firewalls, intrusion detection systems (IDS), and encryption protocols. Document the steps you took to secure your network and any challenges you faced.
- o **Penetration Testing Reports**: Conduct vulnerability assessments and penetration tests on virtual machines or personal websites. Share the results in your portfolio, detailing the vulnerabilities discovered and the methods you used to exploit and fix them.
- o **Incident Response Simulation**: Create a mock incident response scenario where you identify and contain a simulated security breach. Include a step-by-step process of how

you managed the incident, from detection to recovery.

- o **Malware Analysis**: Perform static and dynamic analysis of malware samples in a controlled environment (e.g., virtual machine). Document your findings, including how the malware works and how to defend against it.

**Tip**: Be sure to include **clear documentation** for each project. This could be in the form of **reports**, **presentations**, or even **GitHub repositories**. Employers appreciate candidates who can explain their work in a professional and organized manner.

3. **Build a Personal Website or Blog**

Having an **online presence** is essential in cybersecurity. Building a personal website or blog can help you showcase your projects, certifications, and technical expertise. Use this platform to:

- o **Share Your Portfolio**: Display your projects and skills in an easily accessible format.

- o **Write About Cybersecurity**: Write blog posts or articles about trending cybersecurity topics, tutorials, or case studies. This demonstrates thought leadership and a passion for the industry.
- o **Contribute to Open-Source Projects**: Show your engagement with the community by contributing to open-source security projects. This not only helps you learn but also adds credibility to your portfolio.

4. **Highlight Soft Skills and Certifications**

While technical expertise is essential in cybersecurity, employers also value **soft skills** such as **problem-solving, communication**, and **teamwork**. Highlight any relevant soft skills in your portfolio and provide examples of how you've used these skills in previous work, internships, or volunteer roles.

- o **Certifications**: Showcase any relevant certifications you've earned, such as **CompTIA Security+, CEH, CISSP**, or **Certified Information Security Manager (CISM)**. Include the certification details, the study process, and how you applied what you learned in your projects.

## Demonstrating Your Skills with Real-World Projects and Experiences

Employers want to see how you apply your cybersecurity knowledge in practical situations. Here's how you can demonstrate your skills effectively:

1. **Create a Vulnerability Assessment Report**

   Conduct a **vulnerability assessment** on a sample website or virtual machine and prepare a professional **report** outlining your findings. Include the following:

   o **Vulnerability Details**: Describe the vulnerabilities you found, including their severity and potential impact.
   o **Mitigation Strategies**: Provide recommendations for mitigating the risks you discovered (e.g., patching software, securing network configurations).

235

o **Tools Used**: List the tools you used for your assessment, such as **Nmap**, **Nessus**, or **OpenVAS**.

A well-written vulnerability report is a key part of a cybersecurity portfolio, as it demonstrates both technical and communication skills.

2. **Document a Penetration Testing Engagement**

If you've completed any penetration testing, create a detailed document of your findings. This should include:

o **Test Environment**: Describe the network or application you tested, including any tools or methodologies used (e.g., **Metasploit**, **Burp Suite**, or **Kali Linux**).

o **Attack Scenarios**: Detail the attack vectors you explored, how you exploited vulnerabilities, and the results of each test.

o **Post-Test Analysis**: Provide remediation suggestions for the vulnerabilities you identified.

**Tip**: Ensure that the content is well-organized and formatted. It should be understandable to both technical and non-technical stakeholders.

3. **Contribute to Capture the Flag (CTF) Competitions**

   **Capture the Flag (CTF)** competitions are a great way to demonstrate your skills in a real-world scenario. These competitions present cybersecurity challenges, such as exploiting vulnerabilities, decrypting data, or solving puzzles. By participating in CTFs and posting your achievements on your portfolio, you can showcase your problem-solving abilities and hands-on skills.

   o **Document Your CTF Experience**: Share the challenges you participated in, how you solved them, and any tools or techniques you used. This can be a great addition to your portfolio, as it shows you can think critically under pressure.

**Case Studies of Successful Portfolios and How They Helped Land Jobs in Cybersecurity**

1. **Alex's Journey from IT Support to Security Analyst**

   **Alex** started his career as an IT support technician but wanted to transition into cybersecurity. He created a portfolio that included a **network security project** where he designed and implemented firewalls, a **penetration testing report**, and a **write-up of a recent CTF competition** he participated in. His portfolio also featured blog posts discussing security trends and best practices.

   **Outcome**:
   Alex's comprehensive portfolio demonstrated his hands-on skills, commitment to learning, and passion for cybersecurity. He landed a **security analyst** position at a mid-sized tech company after an interview where his portfolio was a key topic of discussion.

2. **Maria's Transition from Software Development to Penetration Testing**

**Maria**, a software developer, decided to move into penetration testing. She built her portfolio around a **series of penetration tests** she had conducted on her own personal web applications and published detailed reports on her website. She also included a few **write-ups of CTF challenges** and a **malware analysis project**.

**Outcome**:

Maria's portfolio impressed the hiring manager at a cybersecurity firm, who appreciated her technical depth and ability to explain complex topics clearly. She successfully transitioned into a **penetration tester** role, leveraging her software development background to identify security vulnerabilities in web applications.

3. **Tom's Portfolio Led to a Role in Security Management**

**Tom** had several years of experience in IT but wanted to transition into a security management role. He created a portfolio that included a **business impact analysis (BIA)** he had conducted for a client and a **risk management framework** he had

239

implemented in his previous company. He also included a series of blog posts and security strategy recommendations.

**Outcome**:

Tom's portfolio showcased his understanding of the broader aspects of cybersecurity, including risk management and governance. He was hired as a **security manager** at a large financial institution, where he was responsible for overseeing the company's security operations and strategy.

## Conclusion: Building Your Cybersecurity Portfolio for Success

A strong cybersecurity portfolio is an invaluable tool for advancing your career. By showcasing your skills through real-world projects, certifications, and continuous learning, you demonstrate to potential employers that you are capable and passionate about the field. Whether you are just starting out or looking to transition into a more advanced role, your portfolio can be the key to unlocking new career opportunities in cybersecurity.

By following the steps outlined in this chapter, you can build a portfolio that highlights your practical skills, technical knowledge, and ability to solve real-world problems, setting you apart in the competitive cybersecurity job market.

This chapter provides an in-depth look at how to build a strong cybersecurity portfolio, complete with practical examples and real-world stories of professionals who leveraged their portfolios to secure jobs in the industry.

# CHAPTER 21

# DEVELOPING ADVANCED HACKING SKILLS

## Introduction: The Journey from Beginner to Advanced Ethical Hacker

Becoming an ethical hacker requires more than just understanding basic concepts and tools. To truly excel in the field, you must be prepared to tackle complex security challenges, think critically, and continuously improve your skills. As you progress from a beginner to an advanced ethical hacker, you will need to master sophisticated techniques, advanced tools, and real-world attack strategies. This chapter will guide you through the process of advancing your hacking skills, with a focus on hands-on experience with tools like **buffer overflow attacks**, **reverse engineering**, and more. We will also explore real-world examples of advanced hacking techniques used in ethical hacking scenarios.

## How to Progress from Beginner to Advanced Ethical Hacker

1. **Master the Basics**
   Before diving into advanced hacking techniques, it's essential to have a strong foundation in basic cybersecurity concepts. This includes understanding network protocols, operating systems, and fundamental security practices. If you're just starting out, focus on mastering the following areas:

   o **Networking Fundamentals**: Learn how data is transmitted across networks, how devices communicate, and the basics of **IP addressing, DNS, HTTP/S**, and **TCP/IP** protocols.

   o **Operating System Proficiency**: Understand the inner workings of **Linux, Windows**, and **macOS**, as these are the most commonly used operating systems in cybersecurity.

   o **Basic Penetration Testing**: Familiarize yourself with essential penetration testing tools like **Nmap, Wireshark, Burp Suite**, and **Metasploit**. Practice using these tools in controlled environments like **Hack The Box** or **TryHackMe**.

o **Ethical Hacking Principles**: Understand the ethical guidelines for hacking, such as obtaining proper authorization and following responsible disclosure protocols.

2. **Learn Advanced Hacking Techniques**

Once you've gained a solid foundation, it's time to start working with more advanced tools and techniques. Here are some areas to focus on as you progress in your ethical hacking journey:

o **Buffer Overflow Attacks**: Buffer overflow attacks occur when an attacker sends more data into a buffer than it can handle, causing the program to overwrite adjacent memory locations. By exploiting this, attackers can execute arbitrary code, such as gaining unauthorized access or executing malicious commands.

o **Reverse Engineering**: Reverse engineering involves analyzing and deconstructing software to understand how it works, identify vulnerabilities, and manipulate its behavior. Ethical hackers use reverse engineering to find bugs in applications and create patches or workarounds.

244

- o **Exploitation of Advanced Vulnerabilities**: Learn how to exploit complex vulnerabilities, such as **SQL injection, cross-site scripting (XSS), cross-site request forgery (CSRF),** and **race conditions**. These vulnerabilities can be harder to find and exploit but are critical to understanding and mitigating in real-world scenarios.

- o **Advanced Web Application Security**: Web application security requires a deep understanding of web technologies and their associated vulnerabilities. This includes mastering tools like **OWASP ZAP** and **Burp Suite** to discover vulnerabilities in web applications, APIs, and services.

- o **Wireless Network Attacks**: Learn how to exploit wireless networks by targeting weak encryption standards like **WEP** or misconfigurations in **Wi-Fi networks**. Use tools like **Aircrack-ng, Kismet**, and **Reaver** to crack Wi-Fi passwords and analyze network traffic.

3. **Work with Advanced Hacking Tools**

   As you advance, you will need to familiarize yourself

with more sophisticated hacking tools that allow you to perform deeper analysis and manipulation. Some key tools and techniques include:

- o **Buffer Overflow Tools**: Tools like **Immunity Debugger** and **OllyDbg** are used to analyze and manipulate programs with buffer overflow vulnerabilities.

- o **Reverse Engineering Software**: IDA Pro, **Ghidra**, and **Radare2** are popular reverse engineering tools that allow you to deconstruct binaries and understand their underlying code.

- o **Exploit Development**: Learn how to develop custom exploits using frameworks like **Metasploit** and **Core Impact** to simulate real-world attack scenarios.

- o **Advanced Malware Analysis**: Use tools like **Cuckoo Sandbox** and **REMnux** to analyze malicious files and determine their behavior.

---

**Hands-On Experience with Advanced Tools**

1. **Buffer Overflow Attacks**

Buffer overflow attacks allow an attacker to exploit a vulnerability in a program that does not properly handle memory allocation. By overwriting a buffer, an attacker can inject malicious code and gain control over the system.

**Example Scenario**:

- o Suppose a program has an insecure function that copies user input into a fixed-size buffer. If the user input exceeds the buffer's size, the excess data will overwrite adjacent memory, which can lead to unintended behavior, such as code execution.

**Tool to Use**:

- o **Immunity Debugger**: Use this tool to analyze software and identify buffer overflow vulnerabilities. By debugging the application, you can examine how input data is handled and find opportunities to exploit the overflow.

**Real-World**            **Application**:

Buffer overflow attacks have been used to exploit

vulnerabilities in software like **Microsoft Office** and **Adobe Reader**, where attackers could craft malicious files that, when opened, would overflow the buffer and execute arbitrary code.

2. **Reverse Engineering**

Reverse engineering is an essential skill for advanced ethical hackers. By dissecting software, ethical hackers can identify vulnerabilities, uncover hidden malware, and develop strategies for defending against attacks.

**Example Scenario**:

- o You are tasked with analyzing a suspicious executable file that might contain malware. Using reverse engineering techniques, you can analyze the file's code, trace its execution, and uncover malicious behavior, such as unauthorized data exfiltration or privilege escalation.

**Tools to Use**:

248

- **IDA Pro**: A powerful disassembler and debugger used for analyzing binaries. It helps you understand how programs work by transforming machine code into a human-readable format.

- **Ghidra**: A free, open-source reverse engineering tool developed by the NSA. It is used for deconstructing software and identifying vulnerabilities.

**Real-World Application**: Reverse engineering is frequently used to uncover vulnerabilities in proprietary software. For example, in 2017, researchers used reverse engineering to discover vulnerabilities in **Cisco's WebEx** software that allowed attackers to execute arbitrary code remotely.

3. **Advanced Web Application Hacking**

Web applications are often targeted by attackers because they are exposed to the internet, making them an attractive entry point. Mastering web application security is essential for advanced ethical hackers.

**Example Scenario**:

- An attacker discovers that a web application is vulnerable to **SQL injection**, allowing them to inject malicious SQL queries into a login form to bypass authentication and access sensitive data.

**Tools to Use**:

- **Burp Suite**: A powerful web application security testing tool that helps identify vulnerabilities such as **XSS**, **SQL injection**, and **CSRF**.
- **OWASP ZAP**: Another excellent tool for discovering vulnerabilities in web applications, designed for penetration testers to perform automated scans and manual testing.

**Real-World                                Application**:
SQL injection remains one of the most common web application vulnerabilities. In 2018, hackers exploited SQL injection vulnerabilities in **MySQL**

databases to steal millions of customer records from **T-Mobile**.

---

## Real-World Examples of Advanced Hacking Techniques in Ethical Scenarios

1. **The Stuxnet Attack (2010)**

   The **Stuxnet** worm was one of the most sophisticated cyberattacks ever discovered. It was designed to sabotage Iran's nuclear program by infecting industrial control systems (ICS) and causing damage to centrifuges used for uranium enrichment. The worm was a highly targeted attack, using advanced techniques such as **zero-day vulnerabilities**, **rootkits**, and **buffer overflow attacks**.

   **Ethical Hacking Context**: In ethical scenarios, advanced hackers may use similar techniques to test the resilience of industrial control systems. By understanding how **Stuxnet** exploited vulnerabilities, ethical hackers can develop better defenses for critical infrastructure.

251

## 2. The Target Data Breach (2013)

The **Target** data breach was caused by a successful phishing attack that compromised a third-party vendor's credentials. Once inside the network, attackers used advanced techniques, including **lateral movement** and **credential stuffing**, to escalate their privileges and access payment card information.

**Ethical Hacking Context**: Ethical hackers working with retail organizations can use **penetration testing** techniques to simulate such attacks and identify weaknesses in network segmentation, vendor management, and authentication systems.

---

## Conclusion: Advancing Your Hacking Skills

Becoming an advanced ethical hacker requires continuous learning and hands-on experience. By mastering complex hacking techniques, tools, and methodologies, you can become a more effective and skilled professional in the cybersecurity field. Whether you're focusing on **buffer**

**overflow attacks**, **reverse engineering**, or **web application security**, developing advanced skills will help you tackle the most challenging security issues and make a significant impact in the fight against cybercrime.

The journey from beginner to advanced ethical hacker involves persistence, practice, and a commitment to learning new techniques. As you develop your skills, remember to always follow ethical guidelines and work responsibly to help protect systems and networks from malicious attackers.

---

This chapter provides insights into the journey of developing advanced ethical hacking skills, including hands-on experience with complex tools and techniques.

# *CHAPTER 22*

# *THE ROLE OF CYBERSECURITY IN COMPLIANCE AND GOVERNANCE*

**Introduction: The Intersection of Cybersecurity, Compliance, and Governance**

In today's digital world, cybersecurity is not just about protecting data from unauthorized access or malicious attacks. It also involves adhering to **compliance regulations** and **governance frameworks** that ensure organizations meet legal, ethical, and industry-specific standards. Compliance with these regulations is a critical component of an organization's cybersecurity strategy, as failure to do so can lead to severe legal, financial, and reputational consequences.

This chapter will explore how cybersecurity intersects with major regulatory requirements like **GDPR**, **HIPAA**, and **PCI DSS**, discuss why compliance is essential for both companies and cybersecurity professionals, and examine real-world examples of breaches caused by non-compliance.

**How Cybersecurity Intersects with Regulatory Requirements: GDPR, HIPAA, PCI DSS**

1. **General Data Protection Regulation (GDPR)**

   **GDPR** is a regulation established by the European Union (EU) that aims to protect the privacy and personal data of individuals within the EU. It sets strict guidelines on how organizations collect, store, process, and share personal data. GDPR applies to any company that handles the personal data of EU citizens, regardless of where the company is based.

   **Key Cybersecurity Considerations under GDPR**:

   - **Data Protection by Design and by Default**: Organizations are required to implement security measures to protect personal data at every stage of its lifecycle.
   - **Data Subject Rights**: Organizations must ensure that individuals can exercise their rights under GDPR, including the right to access, correct, or delete their personal data.

o **Incident Reporting**: GDPR mandates that data breaches must be reported within **72 hours** of detection to the relevant authorities and affected individuals.

**Cybersecurity Impact**: Organizations must implement robust data security controls (e.g., encryption, access management, and monitoring systems) to meet GDPR requirements and avoid hefty fines.

2. **Health Insurance Portability and Accountability Act (HIPAA)**

**HIPAA** is a U.S. law that governs the security and privacy of healthcare data, particularly in the context of **protected health information (PHI)**. It applies to healthcare providers, insurers, and their business associates who handle PHI.

**Key Cybersecurity Considerations under HIPAA**:

o **Data Encryption**: HIPAA mandates that PHI should be encrypted, both in transit and at rest, to prevent unauthorized access.

- ○ **Access Controls**: Organizations must limit access to PHI to only authorized personnel and maintain a **user authentication system**.
- ○ **Incident Response**: HIPAA requires that healthcare organizations have an incident response plan in place to detect and respond to breaches that may involve PHI.

**Cybersecurity Impact**: To comply with HIPAA, healthcare organizations must implement **strong encryption**, **access control policies**, and **audit logs** to protect sensitive health data.

3. **Payment Card Industry Data Security Standard (PCI DSS)**

**PCI DSS** is a set of security standards designed to ensure that all companies that handle credit card data maintain a secure environment. It applies to any organization that stores, processes, or transmits cardholder data, including merchants, financial institutions, and service providers.

**Key Cybersecurity Considerations under PCI DSS**:

- o **Encryption and Tokenization**: PCI DSS requires that cardholder data be encrypted during transmission and stored securely.

- o **Access Control**: Strict access control policies must be in place to ensure that only authorized personnel can access cardholder data.

- o **Monitoring and Logging**: Organizations must maintain detailed logs of all access to payment card data, along with a robust monitoring system to detect any unauthorized access attempts.

**Cybersecurity Impact**: To meet PCI DSS requirements, organizations must implement encryption, access controls, and regular vulnerability assessments, ensuring that cardholder data remains protected at all times.

---

**Why Compliance Is Important for Both Companies and Cybersecurity Professionals**

1. **For Companies**

- **Avoiding Fines and Penalties**: Non-compliance with regulatory requirements can result in hefty fines. For example, under **GDPR**, organizations can face fines of up to **4% of global annual revenue** or **€20 million**, whichever is greater.

- **Protecting Reputation**: Compliance demonstrates to customers, partners, and investors that an organization is serious about protecting sensitive data, which can enhance trust and improve business relationships.

- **Business Continuity**: Regulatory compliance ensures that organizations have processes in place to manage data security risks, which in turn helps protect business operations from disruptions caused by data breaches.

- **Competitive Advantage**: Companies that comply with industry regulations can position themselves as trusted and secure partners, making them more attractive to customers and clients.

2. **For Cybersecurity Professionals**

o **Ensuring Legal and Ethical Responsibility**: Cybersecurity professionals are responsible for ensuring that organizations adhere to regulatory requirements. This not only protects the organization but also ensures compliance with laws and regulations, which can have legal consequences.

o **Enhancing Career Prospects**: Being knowledgeable about regulatory compliance frameworks such as GDPR, HIPAA, and PCI DSS can make cybersecurity professionals more valuable to employers, as they are seen as experts in safeguarding data and managing compliance risks.

o **Staying Ahead of Emerging Risks**: Compliance regulations often evolve in response to emerging threats, so staying current with the latest regulatory requirements helps cybersecurity professionals stay ahead of new security risks.

**Real-World Examples of Cybersecurity Breaches Due to Non-Compliance**

1. **The Equifax Data Breach (2017)**

   In 2017, **Equifax**, one of the largest credit reporting agencies in the U.S., suffered a massive data breach that exposed the personal information of **147 million people**. The breach occurred because Equifax failed to patch a known vulnerability in the **Apache Struts** framework, which had been disclosed and patched months earlier. While this failure was a technical oversight, it was also a violation of the **PCI DSS** and **GDPR** principles of vulnerability management and timely patching.

   **Consequences**:

   - Equifax faced **$700 million in fines** and settlements, including compensation for affected individuals.
   - The breach severely damaged Equifax's reputation, with many customers losing trust in the company's ability to protect their sensitive data.

261

**Lesson**: Organizations must adhere to compliance requirements related to vulnerability management, especially when dealing with sensitive data like personal and financial information.

2. **The Target Data Breach (2013)**

In 2013, **Target** experienced a data breach that compromised the credit card information of over **40 million customers**. The breach was traced back to a third-party vendor, whose systems were compromised due to inadequate security practices. This breach violated **PCI DSS** requirements related to third-party risk management, network segmentation, and access control.

**Consequences**:

- o Target incurred more than **$200 million in direct costs**, including legal fees, customer compensation, and security improvements.
- o The breach exposed vulnerabilities in Target's supply chain and resulted in a significant loss of consumer trust.

**Lesson**: Third-party risk management is a crucial aspect of compliance, particularly for organizations handling payment card information.

3. **The HealthSouth HIPAA Violation (2015)**

In 2015, **HealthSouth**, one of the largest healthcare providers in the U.S., faced a significant **HIPAA violation** due to inadequate security practices that exposed patients' protected health information (PHI). The breach occurred when the company failed to encrypt data properly, and an unencrypted laptop was stolen containing sensitive patient information.

**Consequences**:

- HealthSouth was **fined $2.8 million** for failing to protect PHI under HIPAA regulations.
- The breach caused reputational damage and prompted a broader discussion about the security of health data.

**Lesson**: Compliance with data protection regulations, such as **HIPAA**, is essential for protecting sensitive healthcare information and avoiding substantial penalties.

## Conclusion: Cybersecurity, Compliance, and Governance in a Digital World

As cyber threats continue to evolve, compliance with regulatory requirements like **GDPR**, **HIPAA**, and **PCI DSS** becomes increasingly vital for organizations seeking to protect their data and ensure business continuity. Cybersecurity professionals play a pivotal role in helping organizations meet these requirements by implementing security controls, managing risk, and responding to incidents promptly.

Adhering to compliance regulations not only helps prevent costly breaches but also strengthens the overall security posture of an organization. For cybersecurity professionals, staying current with the latest regulatory standards and understanding their impact on cybersecurity practices is key to advancing in the field and protecting both the organization and its customers from potential harm.

This chapter covered the intersection of cybersecurity with compliance and governance, highlighting key regulations and real-world examples of breaches caused by non-compliance.

# *CHAPTER 23*

# *WORKING IN CYBERSECURITY CONSULTING*

## Introduction: The Growing Demand for Cybersecurity Consultants

Cybersecurity consulting is one of the most dynamic and in-demand fields in the cybersecurity industry. As businesses face increasingly sophisticated threats, they turn to **cybersecurity consultants** to help assess vulnerabilities, develop security strategies, and implement effective defenses. Cybersecurity consultants bring specialized expertise to help organizations safeguard their networks, data, and systems from potential breaches and attacks.

In this chapter, we'll explore the role of cybersecurity consultants, how to become one, real-world examples of consulting projects, and how to start your own cybersecurity consulting business.

**The Role of Cybersecurity Consultants and How to Become One**

1. **What Do Cybersecurity Consultants Do?**

Cybersecurity consultants provide expert advice to organizations on how to protect their systems, data, and networks from cyber threats. Their role can vary depending on the size and complexity of the organization they work with, but generally, cybersecurity consultants are responsible for:

- **Risk Assessment and Vulnerability Analysis**: Conducting security audits and assessments to identify potential vulnerabilities in an organization's infrastructure, systems, and processes.
- **Security Strategy Development**: Advising on the design and implementation of security strategies and policies that align with industry standards and regulatory requirements.
- **Incident Response**: Assisting organizations in responding to cyber incidents, including

267

data breaches, malware infections, and other security threats.

- o **Compliance Guidance**: Helping businesses comply with relevant cybersecurity regulations, such as GDPR, HIPAA, PCI DSS, and others, by ensuring that security practices align with regulatory requirements.

- o **Security Architecture**: Designing and implementing secure networks, firewalls, and other defense mechanisms to safeguard systems from attacks.

- o **Employee Training**: Educating employees on cybersecurity best practices and creating awareness about common threats like phishing, social engineering, and password management.

2. **How to Become a Cybersecurity Consultant**

Becoming a successful cybersecurity consultant requires a combination of technical expertise, business acumen, and communication skills. Here are the essential steps to follow:

- o **Build a Strong Foundation in Cybersecurity**: Start by gaining

268

foundational knowledge in cybersecurity concepts, including networking, cryptography, firewalls, penetration testing, and threat management. Certifications like **CompTIA Security+, Certified Ethical Hacker (CEH),** or **Certified Information Systems Security Professional (CISSP)** are valuable for building credibility.

o **Gain Practical Experience**: Hands-on experience is crucial. Work in cybersecurity roles such as **security analyst, network administrator,** or **penetration tester** to build your practical skills. Experience in these roles will give you insights into the real-world challenges businesses face regarding cybersecurity.

o **Specialize in a Niche Area**: As you gain experience, consider specializing in a specific area of cybersecurity, such as **cloud security, incident response, risk management,** or **compliance**. Specialization can make you more attractive to potential clients looking for expertise in a specific area.

269

- o **Develop Strong Communication Skills**: As a consultant, you will need to explain complex technical issues to non-technical stakeholders. Strong verbal and written communication skills are essential to ensure your recommendations are understood and acted upon by business leaders.

- o **Stay Up to Date with Trends**: Cybersecurity is an ever-evolving field. Stay informed about the latest threats, technologies, and regulatory changes. Participate in **cybersecurity conferences**, engage with online communities, and take advanced certifications to stay ahead of the curve.

## Real-World Examples of Consulting Projects: Advising Businesses on Security Posture

1. **Risk Assessment and Penetration Testing for a Financial Institution**

**Project Overview**: A cybersecurity consultant was hired by a mid-sized bank to assess its security

270

posture. The consultant conducted a **vulnerability assessment** and **penetration test** to identify weaknesses in the bank's online banking platform and internal systems.

**Consulting Actions**:

- o **Vulnerability Assessment**: The consultant used tools like **Nmap** and **Nessus** to scan for vulnerabilities in the bank's network infrastructure and internal systems.
- o **Penetration Testing**: The consultant performed simulated attacks on the online banking platform to identify potential vulnerabilities, including SQL injection flaws and weak authentication protocols.
- o **Risk Analysis**: After identifying vulnerabilities, the consultant provided a detailed risk analysis and prioritized recommendations for remediation based on the severity of the risks.

**Outcome**:

The bank implemented the consultant's recommendations, including upgrading security

271

protocols, improving authentication processes, and applying patches to critical vulnerabilities. As a result, the bank enhanced its security posture and avoided potential data breaches.

2. **Compliance Consulting for a Healthcare Provider**

**Project Overview**: A healthcare provider sought advice on ensuring compliance with **HIPAA** regulations, especially regarding the protection of **protected health information (PHI)**.

**Consulting Actions**:

- o **Data Security Review**: The consultant conducted a thorough review of the organization's data security practices, focusing on encryption, data storage, and access control.
- o **Gap Analysis**: The consultant identified gaps in the organization's compliance with HIPAA requirements, including inadequate employee training on data security policies.
- o **Remediation Plan**: The consultant developed a comprehensive plan to address

272

compliance gaps, including encrypting sensitive data, enhancing access controls, and implementing regular security audits.

**Outcome**:

The healthcare provider successfully achieved **HIPAA compliance** and improved its security policies, reducing the risk of fines and protecting patient data.

3. **Cloud Security Consulting for a SaaS Company**

**Project Overview**: A **Software-as-a-Service (SaaS)** company wanted to ensure the security of its cloud-based infrastructure and the protection of customer data stored on its servers.

**Consulting Actions**:

- o **Cloud Security Assessment**: The consultant reviewed the company's cloud architecture, focusing on **AWS** security configurations, identity management, and encryption practices.
- o **Security Best Practices**: The consultant provided guidance on implementing best

practices for cloud security, including multi-factor authentication (MFA), encryption at rest and in transit, and secure API management.

○ **Incident Response Planning**: The consultant also helped the company develop an incident response plan specifically tailored to cloud environments.

**Outcome**:

The SaaS company enhanced its cloud security measures, improving its infrastructure's resilience against potential threats and gaining the trust of its customers by ensuring that their data was properly secured.

---

**How to Start Your Own Cybersecurity Consulting Business**

Starting your own cybersecurity consulting business can be a lucrative and rewarding career path, especially if you have the skills, expertise, and passion for helping organizations protect their digital assets. Here are the key steps to get started:

1. **Define Your Niche and Services**

   Decide on the specific services you will offer. Cybersecurity is a broad field, and specializing in a niche area can help differentiate your business. Some common areas of focus for cybersecurity consultants include:

   - Penetration testing and vulnerability assessments
   - Risk management and compliance consulting
   - Cloud security consulting
   - Incident response and disaster recovery
   - Security architecture and design

2. **Build Your Brand and Reputation**

   Establish yourself as an expert in your chosen niche. Build an online presence through a professional website and social media profiles where you can share your knowledge, case studies, and success stories. Engage with the cybersecurity community by contributing to forums, blogs, and conferences.

3. **Obtain Necessary Certifications and Licenses**

While certifications are important for building credibility, depending on your location, you may also need to obtain a business license, tax identification number, and any other local regulatory requirements to legally operate as a consultant.

4. **Network and Find Clients**

Networking is crucial in the consulting business. Attend industry events, reach out to potential clients via LinkedIn, and leverage professional connections to generate leads. You can also advertise your services on job boards, industry-specific platforms, and through referrals.

5. **Set Your Pricing and Contracts**

Determine your pricing model, whether it's hourly, project-based, or retainer. Make sure to establish clear terms in contracts, including service deliverables, timelines, payment structures, and liability clauses.

6. **Stay Updated and Continuously Improve**

Cybersecurity is a fast-evolving field, and staying updated with the latest trends, tools, and techniques is crucial. Regularly update your skills through training and certifications to remain competitive in the consulting space.

## Conclusion: Building a Career in Cybersecurity Consulting

Cybersecurity consulting is a dynamic and rewarding field that offers opportunities to work with a wide range of clients and industries. By gaining experience, mastering key skills, and specializing in a niche area, you can build a successful career as a cybersecurity consultant. Additionally, starting your own consulting business can be a lucrative venture that allows you to provide tailored security solutions to organizations seeking expert guidance.

With the increasing complexity of cyber threats and the growing need for cybersecurity expertise, consulting in this field offers immense potential for growth and success.

This chapter provides insights into the role of cybersecurity consultants, how to become one, and how to start your own cybersecurity consulting business.

# CHAPTER 24

# THE GROWING THREAT OF INSIDER ATTACKS

## Introduction: The Hidden Danger of Insider Threats

When most people think about cybersecurity threats, their minds often turn to external attackers—hackers, cybercriminals, and nation-state actors. However, one of the most dangerous and often overlooked threats comes from within an organization itself. **Insider attacks**—when individuals within an organization exploit their access to compromise sensitive data or systems—are on the rise. These attacks can be harder to detect, and the damage they cause can be far-reaching, especially when trusted employees or contractors are involved.

In this chapter, we will explore **insider threats**, how they differ from external attacks, provide real-world examples of insider attacks and their consequences, and discuss strategies for defending against these threats in your organization.

**Understanding Insider Threats and How They Differ from External Attacks**

### 1. What is an Insider Threat?

An **insider threat** refers to a security risk that originates from within the organization, typically from employees, contractors, or business partners who have access to the organization's internal systems, networks, or data. Unlike external attackers who must breach security defenses to gain access, insiders already have trusted access to systems, making their attacks more difficult to detect.

**Types of Insider Threats**:

- **Malicious Insiders**: These are individuals who intentionally misuse their access to compromise data, steal intellectual property, or cause harm to the organization. Their motivations may include financial gain, revenge, or political motives.
- **Negligent Insiders**: These individuals do not intend to cause harm but may inadvertently expose sensitive information through careless actions, such as sending confidential data to the wrong recipient or falling for phishing scams.

- **Compromised Insiders**: These are insiders whose credentials have been stolen or misused by external attackers. The attackers use the insider's access to infiltrate the organization without raising suspicion.

2. **How Insider Threats Differ from External Attacks**

- **Access**: Insiders typically have legitimate access to sensitive data and systems, which external attackers must work harder to acquire. This makes insider threats more difficult to detect.
- **Intent**: External attackers are usually driven by profit, hacking for financial or political gain, or seeking to damage an organization's reputation. Insiders, however, can be motivated by personal grievances, financial incentives, or even simple carelessness.
- **Detection**: Insider attacks often involve legitimate credentials, making it challenging for security systems to flag them as suspicious. External attacks typically trigger alerts from firewalls, intrusion detection systems, or other security measures.
- **Damage Potential**: Insiders who have intimate knowledge of an organization's systems and

procedures can often cause more targeted and severe damage than external attackers. They can bypass security controls and exfiltrate large volumes of sensitive data.

## Real-World Cases of Insider Attacks and Their Consequences

1. **The Edward Snowden Case (2013)**

One of the most infamous insider attacks in recent history, **Edward Snowden**, a former contractor for the **National Security Agency (NSA)**, stole classified information regarding U.S. government surveillance programs. Snowden had access to sensitive data and used his clearance to download thousands of classified documents, which he later leaked to journalists.

**Consequences**:

- o   The leak caused a massive scandal, damaging the trust between the U.S. government and its allies, and led to widespread public debates over privacy and government surveillance.

o Snowden's actions resulted in major policy changes, including reforms to the U.S. surveillance programs.

o The incident significantly impacted the NSA's ability to operate with discretion and led to the revocation of Snowden's security clearance.

2. **The Target Data Breach (2013)**

In 2013, **Target** experienced a major data breach that exposed the personal and financial data of over 40 million customers. The breach occurred due to the actions of an insider—an employee of a third-party vendor who had privileged access to Target's network. The attacker used this access to install malware on Target's systems, which was used to steal payment card information.

**Consequences**:

o Target faced over $200 million in direct costs due to the breach, including legal fees, customer compensation, and the costs of improving security measures.

o The breach severely damaged Target's reputation, leading to a loss of customer trust.

o Target had to implement enhanced security protocols, including stronger vendor access management and better network segmentation.

3. **The Uber Data Breach (2016)**

In 2016, **Uber** experienced a massive data breach that exposed the personal data of 57 million customers and drivers. The breach occurred after two **contractors** working for Uber gained access to an Amazon Web Services (AWS) account used by the company. They downloaded sensitive data, including names, email addresses, phone numbers, and driver's license numbers. Uber initially attempted to cover up the breach, paying the hackers $100,000 to delete the stolen data and not disclose the breach.

**Consequences**:

o Uber faced regulatory scrutiny and was fined millions of dollars for failing to report the breach promptly, which violated data protection laws.

o The breach led to a public backlash against Uber, damaging its reputation and resulting in lawsuits.

o Uber's executives were forced to resign, and the company was compelled to improve its internal security practices.

## How to Defend Against Insider Threats in Your Organization

1. **Implement Strong Access Control Policies**

   o **Least Privilege Principle**: Ensure that employees and contractors only have access to the systems and data they need to perform their job duties. This minimizes the risk of accidental or intentional data exposure.

   o **Role-Based Access Control (RBAC)**: Assign specific roles to employees based on their job functions, ensuring that access to sensitive data is restricted to those with legitimate business needs.

- o **Separation of Duties**: Ensure that no individual has full control over a critical process or system. For example, an employee who can approve financial transactions should not be the same person who can alter financial records.

2. **Monitor and Audit User Behavior**
   - o **User Activity Monitoring**: Use tools that track user activity on the network and systems. Monitor for unusual behaviors, such as accessing files unrelated to an employee's role, copying large amounts of data, or logging in at odd hours.
   - o **Audit Trails**: Maintain detailed logs of all user actions, especially those involving sensitive data. This allows you to detect suspicious activity and respond quickly if a breach occurs.
   - o **Anomaly Detection**: Implement machine learning-based solutions that can detect deviations from normal user behavior. These solutions can help identify compromised accounts or insiders attempting to exfiltrate data.

3.  **Create a Robust Incident Response Plan**
    - **Insider Threat Detection**: Develop processes for identifying and addressing insider threats as part of your broader incident response plan. This should include detecting abnormal user behavior, investigating suspicious activities, and managing the fallout from an insider attack.
    - **Quick Response and Containment**: When an insider threat is identified, it's crucial to have procedures in place to immediately contain the threat, such as locking down affected systems and restricting access to sensitive data.
    - **Post-Incident Analysis**: After an insider threat is mitigated, perform a thorough post-mortem to understand how the attack occurred, what could have been done differently, and what additional measures should be implemented to prevent future incidents.

4.  **Educate and Train Employees**
    - **Security Awareness Programs**: Educate employees about the risks of insider threats,

including phishing, social engineering, and how to spot suspicious behavior in the workplace. Employees should understand the importance of safeguarding company data and reporting any suspicious activities.

- o **Behavioral Security Training**: Train employees to recognize the signs of malicious behavior in their colleagues and encourage them to report any red flags. Sometimes, employees can detect insider threats before they escalate if they know what to look for.

5. **Conduct Background Checks and Monitor Third-Party Access**

- o **Background Checks**: Conduct thorough background checks on employees and contractors who will have access to sensitive data. This can help identify potential risks before they arise.

- o **Third-Party Risk Management**: Vet contractors and vendors carefully, and continuously monitor third-party access to your systems. Ensure that third parties adhere to the same cybersecurity standards as your internal employees.

## Conclusion: Addressing the Growing Threat of Insider Attacks

Insider threats are one of the most challenging and damaging cybersecurity risks that organizations face. These threats can come from disgruntled employees, careless mistakes, or compromised insiders, and they are harder to detect than external attacks. However, with the right strategies—such as robust access controls, user activity monitoring, incident response planning, and employee training—organizations can significantly reduce their exposure to insider threats.

Given the growing sophistication of cyber threats and the increasing reliance on digital systems, addressing insider threats should be a critical component of any organization's cybersecurity strategy. By fostering a security-conscious culture and implementing proactive security measures, organizations can mitigate the risk posed by insider threats and protect their critical assets.

This chapter provides a comprehensive overview of insider threats, their impact, and strategies for defending against them.

# CHAPTER 25

# THE ETHICS OF CYBERSECURITY

## Introduction: Navigating the Fine Line Between Ethics and Action in Cybersecurity

Cybersecurity is an ever-evolving field that constantly presents ethical dilemmas, especially for ethical hackers and penetration testers. These professionals play a crucial role in identifying vulnerabilities in systems to prevent malicious attacks. However, the very nature of their job—deliberately attempting to break into systems to find weaknesses—raises important ethical and legal questions. How far can you go in testing the security of a system? What happens when an ethical hacker uncovers sensitive data during a penetration test? And what is the role of consent in hacking?

This chapter delves into the **ethical dilemmas of being an ethical hacker**, the **legal implications** of hacking and penetration testing, and **real-world ethical scenarios** in cybersecurity. By exploring these issues, we aim to help cybersecurity professionals understand the fine line between ethical responsibility and unlawful behavior, ensuring they remain on the right side of both ethics and the law.

---

**The Ethical Dilemmas of Being an Ethical Hacker**

1. **Defining Ethical Hacking and Its Boundaries**

   **Ethical hacking** involves the use of hacking techniques to identify and fix security vulnerabilities in systems with the permission of the organization. The core principle of ethical hacking is that hackers should have authorization to perform their actions and operate within the limits set by the organization. However, ethical hackers often face situations where the boundaries between what is ethically acceptable and what is not become unclear.

   **Common Ethical Dilemmas**:

   - **Exceeding Boundaries of Permission**: Sometimes ethical hackers are granted access to test specific systems, but in the process, they may uncover vulnerabilities in other areas of the organization's network or systems. This raises the question: should they go beyond the scope of the original engagement to report or fix these vulnerabilities, or should they limit their testing to what was explicitly allowed?

o **Unintentional Data Exposure**: During a penetration test, ethical hackers may come across sensitive data—such as customer records, credit card numbers, or login credentials—that they are not authorized to access. Even if the goal is to help the organization, ethical hackers must handle this data carefully to avoid ethical and legal violations.

o **Exploiting Vulnerabilities for Educational Purposes**: Ethical hackers sometimes find themselves in a situation where they have discovered a significant vulnerability but are unsure how much information they should share, particularly if the vulnerability has not been made public yet. Should they report it immediately, or should they conduct further research and develop a more comprehensive report?

2. **The Responsibility of Reporting Vulnerabilities**

Ethical hackers are often in possession of privileged information regarding vulnerabilities that could be exploited by malicious hackers. This knowledge comes with significant responsibility:

- o **Responsibility to Report**: Ethical hackers have an ethical obligation to report any vulnerabilities they find in a responsible manner to the organization or appropriate authorities, especially if those vulnerabilities could cause serious harm if exploited.
- o **Handling Sensitive Information**: Ethical hackers must also be careful when handling sensitive data, such as personal information or proprietary company data. While they may come across this information during a test, ethical hackers must ensure it is not used for personal gain or exposed to unauthorized parties.

---

**Legal Implications of Hacking and Penetration Testing**

1. **Legal Boundaries of Ethical Hacking**

While ethical hacking is performed with the intent of improving security, it is still hacking. Unauthorized access to systems, even with good intentions, can result in legal consequences. It's important to understand the legal landscape surrounding hacking and penetration testing.

- o **Authorization**: The most fundamental legal principle governing ethical hacking is that it must be **authorized**. Performing hacking activities without written permission is illegal, even if the hacker intends to find vulnerabilities to protect the organization. This is why penetration testers must have a clearly defined scope of engagement and written consent.

- o **Penetration Testing Contracts**: Legal protections for ethical hackers are typically outlined in contracts between the hacker (or consulting firm) and the organization requesting the test. These contracts should include:

- A **clear scope** defining the systems and networks that can be tested.
- **Liability clauses** that outline the extent of the tester's responsibility.
- **Confidentiality agreements** that ensure the hacker does not disclose sensitive data discovered during the engagement.

2. **Legal Consequences of Unauthorized Hacking**

Unauthorized hacking is a criminal offense in most jurisdictions. Hacking into a system without permission can lead to serious consequences, including:

- o **Criminal Charges**: In many countries, hacking is punishable by law. In the U.S., the **Computer Fraud and Abuse Act (CFAA)** makes unauthorized access to computer systems a federal crime.
- o **Civil Lawsuits**: In addition to criminal penalties, organizations may sue individuals or firms who conduct penetration tests without permission. This can result in significant financial penalties, as well as

reputational damage to the hacker or consulting firm.

**Real-World Example**:

- o **The Gary McKinnon Case (2002)**: Gary McKinnon, a British hacker, gained unauthorized access to 97 U.S. military and NASA computers, believing he was uncovering UFO evidence. Although he acted alone, McKinnon's actions led to significant legal battles between the U.K. and U.S. authorities. McKinnon faced potential extradition and lengthy prison time before being granted immunity. His case highlights the risks of unauthorized hacking and the importance of legal boundaries in cybersecurity work.

3. **Ethical Disclosure vs. Responsible Disclosure**

Once a vulnerability is identified, the ethical hacker faces a key decision: how to disclose it. **Responsible disclosure** means informing the organization or software vendor about the vulnerability in a manner that allows them to fix it before making the issue public. **Ethical disclosure** involves making the vulnerability public, but typically only after a period of time has passed, allowing the responsible party to implement fixes.

- o **Ethical Disclosure**: Ethical hackers should always aim for responsible disclosure, ensuring they give the organization or vendor enough time to resolve the issue before the vulnerability is publicly disclosed. In some cases, hackers may work with vendors to develop patches or fixes for the issue.

- o **Public Disclosure**: If an organization does not act on the disclosed vulnerability, an ethical hacker may choose to disclose it publicly, but this should be done cautiously. Public disclosure of critical vulnerabilities can protect other potential victims but could also have unintended consequences if attackers exploit the vulnerability before a patch is issued.

**Real-World Ethical Scenarios in Cybersecurity**

1. **The Case of the "Good Samaritan" Hacker**

In 2018, a **security researcher** discovered a severe flaw in a major e-commerce platform that exposed customer data. The researcher, aware of the potential risks, tried to report the issue to the company. However, the company ignored the warnings, and the researcher, frustrated by the lack of response, disclosed the vulnerability publicly to raise awareness. While his intentions were to help, the platform did not appreciate the public disclosure, leading to a legal dispute over the legality of the researcher's actions.

**Ethical                    Dilemma**:
Was the researcher in the right for making the vulnerability public? Did he overstep by bypassing the company's internal process? In this case, the researcher acted ethically by trying to protect the public, but the legal implications of bypassing proper disclosure channels remain complex.

2. **The "White Hat" Hacker Who Goes Too Far**

A **penetration tester** was hired by a financial institution to perform a vulnerability assessment. During the test, the consultant identified a weakness in the company's database that could potentially allow an attacker to access sensitive financial data. However, instead of reporting the vulnerability within the agreed-upon scope, the tester accessed the database and began exploring the data to demonstrate the exploit's potential.

**Ethical**                               **Dilemma**:
Even though the tester's intentions were to show the severity of the vulnerability, was it ethical to breach the scope of the engagement by accessing sensitive data without explicit permission? Here, the consultant crossed the line from ethical hacking to overstepping authority, which could have led to legal consequences for both the consultant and the organization.

---

**Conclusion: Navigating Ethical and Legal Challenges in Cybersecurity**

Cybersecurity professionals, especially ethical hackers, often face difficult ethical and legal challenges in their work. Navigating these challenges requires a deep understanding of both the technical and ethical implications of their actions. Ethical hackers must always ensure they have proper authorization, operate within the scope of their engagement, and be mindful of the potential consequences of their actions.

By adhering to ethical guidelines and legal frameworks, cybersecurity professionals can play a crucial role in protecting organizations while avoiding the risks associated with unauthorized or unethical hacking. Transparency, responsible disclosure, and clear communication with clients are key to maintaining ethical standards and ensuring the long-term success of cybersecurity efforts.

---

This chapter covered the ethics of cybersecurity, focusing on the ethical dilemmas faced by ethical hackers, the legal implications of hacking, and real-world ethical scenarios in cybersecurity.

# CHAPTER 26

# CYBERSECURITY CAREER PATHS: FROM ANALYST TO CISO

### Introduction: The Path to Leadership in Cybersecurity

Cybersecurity is one of the fastest-growing fields in the technology sector, with a wide array of career opportunities at every level. Whether you're just starting out as a **junior analyst** or aiming to become a **Chief Information Security Officer (CISO)**, the path to success in cybersecurity is built on a combination of technical expertise, business acumen, and strong leadership skills.

In this chapter, we will explore the various career progression opportunities in cybersecurity, from entry-level roles to senior executive positions like the CISO. We will also discuss how to transition from a junior role to a senior leadership position and provide real-world examples of professionals who have successfully climbed the cybersecurity career ladder.

**Understanding Career Progression in Cybersecurity**

The field of cybersecurity offers a variety of roles, and career progression depends on the skills and experience you gain over time. Below are some common career paths in cybersecurity, with each role offering new challenges, responsibilities, and opportunities for growth.

*1. Entry-Level Roles*

Entry-level roles are the starting point for most cybersecurity professionals. These positions allow individuals to develop foundational skills in cybersecurity and gain hands-on experience working with security technologies, policies, and procedures.

- **Security Analyst**: Security analysts are responsible for monitoring an organization's networks for security threats, conducting vulnerability assessments, and responding to incidents. Analysts may specialize in areas such as **network security**, **endpoint protection**, or **threat intelligence**.
- **SOC Analyst**: A **Security Operations Center (SOC) Analyst** monitors security alerts, investigates incidents, and escalates issues to higher-level teams.

303

They are often the first line of defense against cyber threats and require strong knowledge of **network traffic** and **incident response**.

- **Penetration Tester**: Also known as ethical hackers, penetration testers perform simulated attacks on systems to identify vulnerabilities. They provide detailed reports on security flaws and recommend ways to patch those vulnerabilities.

**Skillsets Needed**: For entry-level roles, knowledge of basic networking, firewalls, encryption, and understanding common security tools (e.g., **Wireshark**, **Nmap**, **Metasploit**) are crucial. Certifications such as **CompTIA Security+** and **Certified Ethical Hacker (CEH)** are often required.

*2. Mid-Level Roles*

As professionals gain experience and expertise in cybersecurity, they can move into more specialized and leadership-oriented roles. These positions involve greater responsibility and require deeper technical and analytical skills.

- **Security Engineer**: Security engineers design, implement, and maintain security systems, such as firewalls, intrusion detection/prevention systems (IDS/IPS), and encryption protocols. They often collaborate with IT teams to ensure that security measures align with the company's infrastructure.

- **Incident Response Specialist**: Incident response specialists focus on investigating and mitigating cybersecurity breaches. They handle the aftermath of attacks, conducting forensic analysis and working to prevent future incidents.

- **Cybersecurity Consultant**: Consultants provide organizations with expert advice on improving their cybersecurity posture. They may assist with vulnerability assessments, compliance audits, or help organizations design secure networks.

- **Risk Manager**: Risk managers focus on identifying, assessing, and mitigating cybersecurity risks to protect an organization's assets and reputation. They ensure that security practices comply with regulatory requirements and help reduce the likelihood of data breaches.

**Skillsets Needed**: In mid-level roles, professionals need expertise in specialized areas, such as **network security**,

**penetration testing, cryptography**, and **security architecture**. Strong understanding of **risk management frameworks** (e.g., **NIST, ISO 27001**) and industry-specific regulations is also crucial. Certifications like **CISSP, CISM**, and **CISA** become increasingly important.

*3. Senior-Level Roles*

Senior roles require a combination of advanced technical knowledge, leadership capabilities, and strategic thinking. These professionals are responsible for overseeing large-scale security operations and shaping an organization's cybersecurity strategy.

- **Security Architect**: Security architects design and implement security frameworks for the entire organization. They assess security needs, develop secure network architectures, and ensure that security controls are integrated into all systems.

- **Security Operations Manager**: These managers lead teams within a **Security Operations Center (SOC)** or an incident response unit. They oversee daily operations, ensure the effectiveness of security measures, and manage resources to respond to threats.

- **Cybersecurity Director**: Directors are responsible for developing and implementing cybersecurity strategies at the organizational level. They oversee the security operations, budget, and staffing for their department and often work with other departments to align security with overall business goals.

**Skillsets Needed**: Senior-level roles require deep expertise in **security architecture**, **incident management**, and **compliance**. Leadership, project management skills, and the ability to make data-driven decisions are also essential. Certifications such as **CISSP**, **CISM**, and **CISA** are often prerequisites for these roles.

*4. Executive Roles (CISO)*

The **Chief Information Security Officer (CISO)** is the highest-ranking cybersecurity executive in an organization. The CISO is responsible for the overall security strategy, risk management, compliance, and incident response of the organization. They work closely with other C-level executives to align cybersecurity efforts with business objectives.

- **CISO**: The CISO oversees the organization's entire cybersecurity program, from risk management to incident response, and works to ensure the company meets regulatory compliance standards. The CISO is also responsible for managing relationships with stakeholders, such as external auditors and government regulators.

**Skillsets Needed**: As a CISO, you need a blend of deep technical expertise and strategic business knowledge. Leadership skills are essential, as well as the ability to communicate complex security concepts to non-technical stakeholders. Experience in **board-level communication**, **financial management**, and **organizational leadership** is critical.

**Certifications**: Senior executives often hold certifications like **CISSP, CISM, CISA**, and **Certified Chief Information Security Officer (CCISO)**.

---

**How to Transition from a Junior Analyst Role to a Senior Executive Role, Like CISO**

1. **Develop a Strong Technical Foundation**

Begin your career by mastering the core technical skills needed for entry-level roles, such as network security, risk assessment, and ethical hacking. As you progress, deepen your expertise in specialized areas like **cloud security**, **cryptography**, and **incident response**.

2. **Gain Hands-On Experience in Real-World Environments**

Experience is crucial in cybersecurity. Look for opportunities to work on real-world projects, whether through internships, volunteer opportunities, or full-time positions. Take part in **penetration testing**, **incident response** simulations, and **risk assessments** to build practical skills.

3. **Focus on Certifications and Continuous Learning**

Earning industry-recognized certifications is critical to advancing in your cybersecurity career. Certifications like **CISSP**, **CISM**, and **CISA** demonstrate your expertise and commitment to the field, and they are often required for mid-level and senior positions.

4. **Develop Leadership Skills and Strategic Thinking**

Transitioning into senior roles requires strong leadership and business acumen. Start by taking on leadership roles within your team, such as **team lead** or **project manager**. Focus on developing skills in **communication**, **risk management**, and **business strategy** to prepare for executive positions.

5. **Build a Network and Seek Mentorship**

Building a professional network and seeking mentorship from experienced cybersecurity professionals is essential for career growth. Engage with the cybersecurity community through conferences, webinars, and online forums. A mentor can provide valuable advice, guidance, and insight into how to advance to higher positions.

6. **Gain Experience in Risk Management and Governance**

Senior roles, particularly those in cybersecurity leadership, require a solid understanding of **risk management**, **compliance**, and **governance frameworks**. Familiarize yourself with frameworks like **NIST** and **ISO 27001**, and gain experience working on compliance initiatives to strengthen your qualifications for senior positions.

---

**Real-World Examples of Professionals Who Climbed the Cybersecurity Career Ladder**

1. **Example 1: From SOC Analyst to CISO**

   **David** started his career as a **SOC analyst** monitoring security alerts and investigating incidents. Over time, he moved into roles as a **security engineer** and then a **security architect**, where he developed security strategies and designed secure systems. David's leadership skills and deep technical expertise eventually led to his promotion as the **CISO** of a mid-sized financial institution, where he now oversees the entire cybersecurity strategy for the organization.

2. **Example 2: From Penetration Tester to Cybersecurity Consultant**

**Sarah** began as a **penetration tester** and built a reputation for her ability to identify complex vulnerabilities in large-scale enterprise networks. After gaining several certifications like **CEH** and **CISSP**, Sarah transitioned into a **cybersecurity consultant**, helping businesses develop security policies and improve their overall security posture. Today, Sarah runs her own consulting firm, providing high-level advisory services to top-tier companies.

3. **Example 3: From Risk Analyst to CISO**

**John** started his cybersecurity career as a **risk analyst**, focusing on vulnerability assessments and compliance. He then moved into roles in **security governance** and **risk management**. After years of building expertise in **regulatory compliance** and **security strategy**, John was promoted to the **CISO** of a multinational corporation, where he now oversees a global team responsible for the organization's cybersecurity operations.

**Conclusion: Navigating Your Path to Success in Cybersecurity**

The cybersecurity industry offers a wide range of career paths, from technical roles like **security analyst** to executive positions such as **CISO**. The key to progressing through these roles is continuous learning, hands-on experience, and developing both technical and leadership skills. Whether you aspire to become a **CISO**, a **consultant**, or a **security engineer**, the journey requires hard work, dedication, and a commitment to staying up-to-date with the latest trends and technologies.

By following the right steps and taking proactive measures to enhance your skills and knowledge, you can successfully climb the cybersecurity career ladder and achieve your professional goals.

---

This chapter provides an overview of career progression in cybersecurity, offering practical advice and real-world examples for moving from a junior analyst role to senior executive positions.

# CHAPTER 27

# THE FUTURE OF CYBERSECURITY CAREERS

## Introduction: Adapting to the Future of Cybersecurity

As cyber threats become more sophisticated and pervasive, the field of cybersecurity is undergoing rapid transformation. New technologies, emerging threats, and evolving regulatory requirements are shaping the future of cybersecurity careers. To remain relevant and effective, cybersecurity professionals must continuously evolve their skills, embrace new technologies, and understand the emerging trends that will define the future of the industry.

This chapter will explore **emerging trends in cybersecurity**, the **future skill sets** needed for cybersecurity professionals, and strategies for **staying ahead** in the ever-changing landscape of cybersecurity.

## Emerging Trends in Cybersecurity: Cloud Security, IoT Security, Quantum Computing

1. **Cloud Security**

The migration of businesses and services to the **cloud** has become a dominant trend, creating new challenges and opportunities in cybersecurity. As organizations store more critical data and applications on cloud platforms, securing these environments has become a priority.

- o **Why It Matters**: Cloud platforms offer scalability, flexibility, and cost savings, but they also introduce unique security challenges, including **data breaches**, **insecure APIs**, and **misconfigured cloud settings**. As more organizations adopt cloud services, cloud security experts will be in high demand to ensure that data is protected and regulatory requirements are met.

- o **Emerging Focus Areas**:
  - **Cloud-native security tools**: Tools designed specifically to secure cloud environments, such as **CASBs (Cloud Access Security Brokers)** and **Cloud Security Posture Management (CSPM)** tools.

315

- **Zero Trust Architecture (ZTA)**: Emphasizing strict identity and access management controls, Zero Trust frameworks are increasingly being adopted for cloud security, focusing on "never trust, always verify" principles.

2. **IoT Security**

The **Internet of Things (IoT)** continues to grow, with billions of devices being connected to the internet, from smart homes and wearables to industrial control systems. However, many of these devices lack robust security measures, making them prime targets for cybercriminals.

- **Why It Matters**: IoT devices often have limited computational power, making it difficult to implement strong security controls. Furthermore, many of these devices are deployed in **critical infrastructure**, such as energy grids, healthcare systems, and transportation networks, increasing the potential consequences of a successful attack.
- **Emerging Focus Areas**:

- **Device Authentication and Encryption**: Ensuring that IoT devices are properly authenticated and that data transmitted between devices is encrypted to prevent unauthorized access.

- **Edge Security**: As IoT devices generate massive amounts of data, securing edge computing environments—where data is processed near the source—becomes crucial for mitigating risks.

3. **Quantum Computing and Its Impact on Cybersecurity**

**Quantum computing** is an emerging field that has the potential to revolutionize computing by solving complex problems at speeds far beyond traditional computers. However, quantum computing also poses significant challenges to current encryption techniques, threatening the security of encrypted data.

- **Why It Matters**: Quantum computers could potentially break existing encryption

317

methods, such as **RSA** and **ECC (Elliptic Curve Cryptography)**, by using **Shor's Algorithm** to factor large numbers efficiently. As quantum computing becomes more viable, cybersecurity professionals will need to adapt to protect sensitive data.

o **Emerging Focus Areas**:

- **Quantum-Resistant Algorithms**: The development of **post-quantum cryptography** is essential for ensuring that encryption standards remain secure in a future dominated by quantum computers. Professionals will need to understand and implement these quantum-resistant algorithms.

- **Quantum Key Distribution (QKD)**: QKD is an emerging technique for securing communication channels using the principles of quantum mechanics. It ensures that intercepted keys cannot be used to decrypt communications, making it vital for future cybersecurity systems.

318

## The Future Skill Sets Needed for Cybersecurity Professionals

### 1. Cloud Security Expertise

As more organizations transition to cloud environments, cybersecurity professionals will need to master cloud security concepts and tools. Knowledge of **cloud service providers** (AWS, Azure, Google Cloud), **cloud-native security solutions**, and the ability to secure cloud infrastructures will be essential.

- **Skills to Develop**:
  - Familiarity with **cloud security architectures** (e.g., AWS Well-Architected Framework, Azure Security Center).
  - Expertise in **cloud compliance standards** (e.g., SOC 2, ISO 27001).
  - Understanding of **container security** (e.g., Docker, Kubernetes) and securing serverless environments.

319

## 2. IoT Security Skills

With the exponential growth of IoT devices, there will be a demand for professionals who specialize in securing these devices and the networks that connect them. IoT security experts will need to understand both the hardware and software aspects of IoT systems.

- o **Skills to Develop**:
    - Proficiency in **device authentication protocols** and **data encryption** techniques for IoT.
    - Knowledge of **IoT security frameworks** and **vulnerability assessments** for devices.
    - Familiarity with securing the **IoT supply chain**, ensuring that both hardware and software meet security standards.

## 3. Cryptography and Post-Quantum Security

As quantum computing poses a threat to current cryptographic techniques, cybersecurity professionals will need to develop expertise in **post-**

**quantum cryptography** and new encryption technologies designed to withstand the computational power of quantum machines.

- o **Skills to Develop**:
  - Familiarity with **quantum-resistant encryption algorithms** (e.g., lattice-based cryptography).
  - Understanding of the **quantum computing landscape** and its implications for cybersecurity.
  - Knowledge of emerging **quantum key distribution** (QKD) systems for secure communications.

4. **AI and Machine Learning in Cybersecurity**

Artificial Intelligence (AI) and Machine Learning (ML) are playing an increasing role in cybersecurity, particularly in automating threat detection, incident response, and malware analysis. Professionals will need to learn how to leverage AI/ML tools to enhance their security operations.

- o **Skills to Develop**:

- Understanding of **AI-driven threat detection** tools, such as anomaly detection and behavior analysis.
- Familiarity with **machine learning algorithms** used to detect zero-day attacks and advanced persistent threats (APTs).
- Expertise in using **AI** to automate routine security tasks, such as patch management and log analysis.

5. **Security Automation and Orchestration**

As the volume and complexity of security data continue to increase, automation will be crucial for responding to threats in real time. Professionals who can develop, deploy, and manage **security automation tools** will be in high demand.

- o **Skills to Develop**:
    - Proficiency in **Security Orchestration, Automation, and Response (SOAR)** tools.
    - Understanding of **security automation frameworks** and how

they integrate with existing security tools (e.g., SIEM, IDS/IPS).

- Experience in automating **incident response workflows** and integrating threat intelligence into automated systems.

---

**How to Stay Ahead in the Constantly Evolving Field of Cybersecurity**

1. **Continuous Education and Certifications**

Cybersecurity is an ever-changing field, and the best way to stay ahead is through continuous learning. Earning certifications that reflect the latest trends and technologies will help you remain competitive. Key certifications to focus on include:

- ○ **CISSP (Certified Information Systems Security Professional)** for broad security knowledge.
- ○ **CCSP (Certified Cloud Security Professional)** for cloud security expertise.

323

- o **CISM (Certified Information Security Manager)** for those pursuing leadership roles.
- o **Certified Ethical Hacker (CEH)** and **CompTIA Security+** for foundational cybersecurity knowledge.
- o **Post-Quantum Cryptography Certifications** as the industry begins to embrace quantum-resistant encryption.

2. **Stay Informed About Industry Trends**

Keep up-to-date with the latest threats, technologies, and security practices by reading industry blogs, attending webinars and conferences, and engaging with the cybersecurity community. Some valuable resources include:

- o **SANS Institute** for training and certifications.
- o **Dark Reading** and **KrebsOnSecurity** for the latest news on threats and vulnerabilities.
- o **Black Hat** and **DEF CON** for security conferences where professionals showcase the latest research.

3. **Hands-On Practice and Labs**

In addition to formal education, hands-on experience is crucial in cybersecurity. Platforms like **TryHackMe**, **Hack The Box**, and **Cuckoo Sandbox** offer virtual labs where you can practice your skills in penetration testing, malware analysis, and security operations.

4. **Build a Strong Network**

Networking with other cybersecurity professionals can provide insights, job opportunities, and collaborations. Join forums, attend cybersecurity meetups, and engage with peers on platforms like **LinkedIn**, **Reddit's /r/cybersecurity**, or **Twitter**.

## Conclusion: Preparing for the Future of Cybersecurity

The future of cybersecurity holds immense promise and challenges. As new technologies emerge, the role of cybersecurity professionals will continue to evolve. By embracing trends like **cloud security**, **IoT security**, and **quantum computing**, and developing the necessary skill sets in AI, automation, and cryptography, professionals can position themselves for success.

Staying ahead in the cybersecurity field requires a combination of **continuous learning**, **hands-on experience**, and an understanding of the latest industry trends. By being proactive and adaptable, you can not only survive but thrive in the rapidly changing world of cybersecurity.

www.ingramcontent.com/pod-product-compliance
Lightning Source LLC
LaVergne TN
LVHW051431050326
832903LV00030BD/3021